YORK NOTES

General Editors: Professor A.N. Jeffares (*University of Stirling*) & Professor Suheil Bushrui (*American University of Beirut*)

William Shakespeare

HENRY IV PART 1

Notes by F.H. Mares

BA (DURHAM) B LITT (OXFORD) MA (ESSEX)
*Honorary Research Associate in English,
University of Adelaide*

LONGMAN
YORK PRESS

The illustrations of The Globe Playhouse are from
The Globe Restored in Theatre: A Way of Seeing by
Walter C. Hodges, published by Oxford University
Press. © Oxford University Press

YORK PRESS
Immeuble Esseily, Place Riad Solh, Beirut.

LONGMAN GROUP UK LIMITED
Longman House, Burnt Mill, Harlow,
Essex CM20 2JE, England
Associated companies, branches and representatives
throughout the world

© Librairie du Liban 1980

First published 1980
Ninth impression 1991

ISBN 0-582-02270-3

Produced by Longman Group (FE) Ltd.
Printed in Hong Kong

Contents

Part 1

Introduction

Life of William Shakespeare

William Shakespeare was baptised in the parish church at Stratford-upon-Avon on 26 April 1564. He died on 23 April 1616, and it is often assumed that this was his fifty-second birthday. April 23 is the day of St George, the patron saint of England, which makes the guess that it was Shakespeare's birthday more attractive. He was the eldest son of John Shakespeare and his wife Mary Arden; two daughters, who both died in infancy, were born before him, and there were five later children. At the time of William's birth John was a prominent businessman in Stratford. He belonged to the Guild of the Glovers, and his business probably extended from glove-making to dealing in wool and leather, all the processes of tanning, and even to making harness and saddles. There are suggestions that he was also involved in farming and butchery—trades which are related to the supply of the leather-worker's raw materials. His wife Mary came from a slightly higher social class: John Shakespeare's father, Richard, was a tenant farmer, and Mary Arden was the daughter of his landlord.

The baptism of William's younger brothers and sisters are, like his own, recorded: Gilbert (1566), Joan (1569), Anne (1571), Richard (1574) and Edmund (1580). The last followed his brother to London and became an actor, but he died in 1607. Only Joan Shakespeare, who married William Hart, lived longer than William.

At the time of William's birth John Shakespeare was already a leading member of his community, a burgess of Stratford, and in 1568 he was made High Bailiff or Mayor. Soon after this, though, a spell of bad times seems to have begun for him, and the family fortunes declined. He had apparently not been attending meetings of the Stratford Council for about ten years when he was finally removed from its membership in 1586. Of how William spent his childhood there is absolutely no record, but it is a safe assumption that he was sent to the Stratford Grammar school: as a burgess of the town John Shakespeare was entitled to free schooling for his children. At the school William would have learned Latin, and begun to stock his memory with the classical myths and history that were an essential part of grammar-school education. This knowledge is plain from many allusions in his work. Long after he was dead and famous, legends began to accumulate about his youth. He is said to have assisted his father as a butcher, and when he killed a calf he did it in the 'high Roman fashion' with a funeral oration over the sacrificed beast. He is said to have been in trouble for poaching deer on the Lucy estate at Charlecote, near Stratford, and in revenge to have lampooned Sir Thomas Lucy as Justice Shallow in *2 Henry IV*; but none of this can be documented.

What is certain is that at the end of 1582 William Shakespeare was married to Anne (or Agnes) Hathaway. Shakespeare applied on 27 November 1582 for a special licence. He was under age, and he requested that the marriage proceed after only one calling of the banns, instead of the usual three. This was to allow the marriage to take place before Advent (the period including the four Sundays before Christmas and extending to Epiphany, 6 January). During the Advent season marriage could not be celebrated. Susanna, daughter to William Shakespeare, was baptised on 26 May 1583, so the motive for a hasty marriage seems clear. But the licence was for Shakespeare to marry Anne Whately of Temple Grafton, and Anne Hathaway came from Shottery, a quite different village, in a different direction from Stratford. It may be no more than a clerk's confusion, but it may be a hint of a more tangled story. The day after the application for the licence two worthy citizens of Shottery placed a bond of £40 (a large sum in those days) with the Bishop of Worcester that there would be no impediment to the marriage of William Shakespeare and Anne Hathaway. He was eighteen and she twenty-six. Twins, Hamnet and Judith, were baptised on 2 February 1585, but there were no later children. Hamnet died in 1596, but both the daughters married and survived their father.

There is no evidence of when Shakespeare left Stratford and went to London, or of how he came to be an actor, but it is clear that he was established there with quite a reputation by 1592. He can be traced as living in London until 1608, and there is no evidence that he was a regular resident in Stratford before 1612. All of this, combined with the curious legacy of his 'second-best bed' to his wife and the probability that Anne never lived anywhere but in Stratford, has been taken as evidence of an unhappy marriage and early estrangement. It is not conclusive, and is mostly capable of alternative explanation. It has been suggested that the untimely pregnancy was the outcome of a 'troth-plight' marriage (a declaration of intention before witnesses) later given the Church's blessing. This was a known and legitimate practice in Elizabethan England. Specifically to leave his wife his second-best bed was not a bitter final joke at her expense, but the tender thought of a dying man. This was the bed William and Anne would have shared (as the best bed was doubtless reserved for visitors), and it is added specifically to the one-third share of her husband's estate to which Anne was in any case entitled. These explanations may seem like special pleading, but it is plain anyway that Shakespeare maintained connections in Stratford and bought property there in a way that suggested that he had every intention of returning—and that is what he did. By 1612 he was wealthy enough to retire to New Place, a large house which he had bought in 1597. There was only one bigger house in Stratford, and New Place was grand enough to be the resting-place of Queen Henrietta Maria for two days in 1643 when she was on her way to join King Charles at Oxford during the Civil War. By the time he was forty-eight Shakespeare was a wealthy man. He may also have been a sick one, for he died four years later—but there is no evidence for this.

Apart from records of births, marriages and deaths, the documentary evidence we have about the Shakespeare family is mainly legal and commercial. William was a good businessman, buying wisely and not spending extravagantly, and he seems to have paid his debts. For the period in which he lived he was involved in very little litigation. Only Philip Henslowe, who endowed Dulwich College, seems to have made more money out of the theatre than Shakespeare. Henslowe was manager of the Admiral's Men, the most successful London theatre company, after the Lord Chamberlain's Men (later the King's Men), the company to which Shakespeare belonged. Of those contemporaries whose reputation today is nearest his own, Christopher Marlowe (1564–93) died young and violently, and Ben Jonson (1572–1637) who succeeded him as major writer for the King's Men, and whose reputation exceeded Shakespeare's at least until the eighteenth century, died old, sick and forgotten, dependent on pensions and sinecures that were not always paid.

But the knowledge that Shakespeare looked after his money does not tell us much about the man. In 1596 Shakespeare's father's declining fortunes were shored up with the grant of a coat of arms and the formal right to call himself a 'Gentleman': it is almost certain that William paid the quite substantial fees involved, so perhaps we may assume that he was a snob—or at least that he valued title and position, as well as money. The terms of his will in which he left to Susanna the bulk of his property (and it was considerable) suggest that he desired to found a family, a dynasty. From Susanna the property was to pass 'to the first son of her body lawfully issuing and to the heirs males of the body of the said first son lawfully issuing . . .'. Only after all possible sons by Susanna were exhausted were the possible sons of Shakespeare's only grandchild at the time of his death—Susanna's daughter Elizabeth—to inherit. And only after them were the possible sons of his younger daughter Judith to inherit. If Shakespeare did have this dynastic design it was in vain: neither Elizabeth nor the three sons born to Judith after their grandfather's death had any children. William Shakespeare's line was extinct.

There are a few very personal comments on Shakespeare that survive. In 1592 Shakespeare was attacked in a pamphlet written on his deathbed by the pamphleteer and playwright Robert Greene (1560–92) and put through the press by a minor dramatist, Henry Chettle (d. 1607), who later made a handsome apology:

> I am as sorry as if the original fault had been my fault, because myself have seen his demeanour, no less civil than he excellent in the quality he professes. Besides, divers of worship have reported his uprightness of dealing, which argues his honesty, and his facetious grace in writing, which approves his art.

Seven years after Shakespeare's death his colleagues Heminges and Condell published his plays in a collected edition— the 'First Folio' of 1623—and spoke warmly of their dead friend; and Ben Jonson, who was usually rather more given to praise of himself than other people, contributed a fine poem of eulogy to the same volume. In his *Timber; or Discoveries made upon Men and Matter* (1640) Jonson has a more personal comment:

> I loved the man, and do honour his memory, on this side idolatry, as much as any. He was indeed honest, and of an open and free nature; had an excellent fancy, brave notions and gentle expressions.

The one thing that everybody knows about Shakespeare is his work: thirty-seven or thirty-eight plays (for not all the plays attributed to him are everywhere accepted as his); the two long poems, *Venus and Adonis* and *The Rape of Lucrece*; the Sonnets; *The Phoenix and the Turtle* and a few other poems. Here, certainly, it might be thought, we shall find the man, his attitudes, his beliefs, his ideas. And no doubt this is true in some sense, but the interpretation is difficult, particularly with a dramatic writer. All the characters in the plays speak for themselves and not necessarily for their author. It is ironic that some of the most notable passages of moral wisdom (if we are to judge by frequency of quotation) come from characters by no means admirable. Iago, the villain in *Othello*, in a context clearly hypocritical, says, 'Who steals my purse steals trash'. Even the Sonnets, which seem to express deeply felt experience and tell a story in the voice of the poet himself, may be another dramatic manifestation. There is no agreement on the identity of the 'Fair Youth' or the 'Dark Lady' or the 'Rival Poet', though there are many candidates. There is still debate on what, exactly, was the relation between these persons, and it is quite possible that the 'I' of the sequence does not speak directly of Shakespeare's actual personal experience. It has been wisely said that what we find when we read Shakespeare is not so much a record of his experiences as the truth of our own, set down clearly for the first time.

The poet John Keats (1792–1821) described 'a poet' as:

the most unpoetical of anything in existence; because he has no Identity—he is continually infor[ming] and filling some other Body—the Sun, the Moon, the Sea and Men and Women who are creatures of impulse are poetical and have about them an unchangeable attribute— but the poet has none; no identity—he is certainly the most unpoetical of all God's Creatures. (Letter to Woodhouse, 27 October 1818)

After all the researches of scholars and the speculations of biographers in the past four hundred years Shakespeare remains a mystery, a man with no clear identity.

Shakespeare's theatre

How Shakespeare first became an actor and playwright is not known, but by some time in 1594 he had become associated with the company of players known as Lord Hunsdon's, or more commonly, the Lord Chamberlain's Men. Henry Carey, first Lord Hunsdon and the Queen's cousin, became Lord Chamberlain in 1585 and was succeeded in that office by his son. This company was probably re-formed in 1594: the plague had been bad in London in 1593 and the acting companies had had a very hard time. The Chamberlain's Men then emerged as the best of the acting companies. Their supremacy was recognised by royal patronage when James I came to the throne in 1603 and they became the King's Men, and they maintained this dominant position until the closing of the theatres in 1642. The patronage enjoyed by all the companies was a kind of protection and, by the end of the sixteenth century, not much more than a legal fiction. The law classed actors with 'rogues and vagabonds' unless they were the servants of some person of power or rank. Their public performances were nominally a way of keeping in training for the infrequent occasions when they might be called upon to entertain their master. For the King's Men, of course, such calls could be quite frequent, for James I and his wife Anne of Denmark were fond of theatrical entertainments. With the King's Men were associated the best dramatists—not only Shakespeare, but Ben Jonson, Francis Beaumont (1584–1616) and John Fletcher (1579–1625)—and the best actors, in particular, Richard Burbage the tragedian, and such famous clowns as Will Kemp and Robert Armin. When a payment was made to this company for two plays performed at court in the Christmas season of 1594 the payment was made jointly to Richard Burbage, William Shakespeare and William Kemp, which suggests that Shakespeare was a leading member and senior share-holder. His reputation must have been high.

The King's Men provided a remarkably stable group in a profession that has always been precarious. There was a three-tier system within the company. First came the 'sharers': these were the leading members, with money invested in the company (and consequently taking a 'share' of the receipts). Then there were the journeymen—mature actors and other professionals of the theatre—who worked for wages. Finally there were the boys, apprentices learning the trade of acting, who, before their voices broke at puberty, played the women's parts. There were no professional women in the Elizabethan theatre.

Where other companies tended to break up or (like the Admiral's Men with Philip Henslowe) fall under the domination of a particular

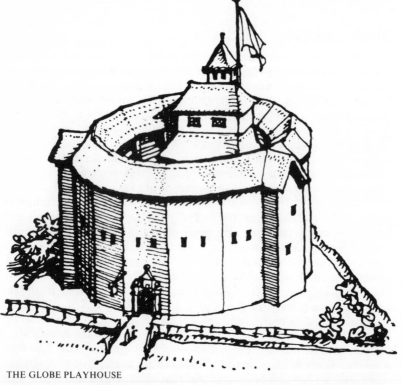

THE GLOBE PLAYHOUSE

The theatre, originally built by James Burbage in 1576, was made of wood (Burbage had been trained as a carpenter). It was situated to the north of the River Thames on Shoreditch in Finsbury Fields. There was trouble with the lease of the land, and so the theatre was dismantled in 1598, and reconstructed 'in another forme' on the south side of the Thames as the Globe. Its sign is thought to have been a figure of the Greek hero Hercules carrying the globe. It was built in six months, its galleries being roofed with thatch. This caught fire in 1613 when some smouldering wadding, from a cannon used in a performance of Shakespeare's *Henry VIII*, lodged in it. The theatre was burnt down, and when it was rebuilt again on the old foundations, the galleries were roofed with tiles.

financier, Shakespeare's company maintained a collective management. Will Kemp withdrew, probably before 1600, but Shakespeare and Burbage remained for all their working lives, and were joined by others equally stable. Shakespeare's share in the company, while he was actively involved with it, ranged from about one-sixth to one-tenth, as others came and went.

The Lord Chamberlain's/King's Men also kept control of their own theatre.In this also they differed from most of the other companies, who were usually tenants of an entrepreneur or financier. James Burbage, the father of Richard, was responsible for building the first theatre in London. This was the Theatre in Shoreditch, north-east of the city, and it was here that Shakespeare's company originally worked. In 1598— after, it appears, a quarrel with their ground-landlord—they demolished the theatre and re-erected it on a new site on the south side of the Thames, in Southwark, and called it the Globe. This building was burned down in 1613 when Shakespeare's *Henry VIII* was being performed, but was soon rebuilt. In 1608 the King's Men acquired a second theatre in the old monastic buildings of the Blackfriars. This was a roofed building, where plays could be given in all weathers and at all seasons of the year. It catered for a more select audience, and charged higher admission prices.

The Globe was an 'outdoor' theatre. It was a circular or polygonal building, enclosing a central courtyard. The courtyard was open, but was surrounded by three tiers of roofed galleries. The interior diameter of the courtyard was probably about eighteen metres, and the total diameter of the building about twenty-six metres. A stage, raised about a metre or a metre and a half, projected from one side wall about to the middle of the yard. The audience in the roofed galleries and the 'understanders' in the yard—so called punningly because they stood below the level of the stage—surrounded the stage on three sides. The fourth side contained doors for entrances and exits and some kind of enclosed area or 'discovery space'. In *1 Henry IV*, II.4.293, the Prince says to Falstaff, 'Go hide thee behind the arras'. Later on (l.520) when the Sheriff has gone Falstaff is revealed sleeping 'behind the arras'. Many discussions of the Elizabethan theatre refer to this 'discovery space' as 'the inner stage' and assume that there was a curtained recess of some size at the back of the acting area. This view is not so confidently held now as it was twenty or thirty years ago, but clearly the scene requires a space screened by a curtain, and large enough for Falstaff to be revealed at l.520, stretched out asleep. When Falstaff is directed to hide behind the arras the Prince instructs the rest of his companions to 'walk up above'. Whether they provide comic business by observing the Prince's interview with the Sheriff from 'above', in full view of the audience, is not clear in this scene, but they may have done so. It is in any case clear from many plays that the Elizabethan theatre had an 'upper stage', above the main acting area, which was used in appropriate situations. So for example in *Henry V*, III.3, at the seige of Harfleur, it is likely that the defenders of the city appeared 'above', on the 'upper stage', while King Henry urged them to surrender from the main stage level. The 'upper stage' in that case served as the walls of the besieged town. The area behind the stage was referred to generally as the 'tiring-house' (dressing-room) and it would have served the same purposes as the 'backstage' areas of a modern theatre, including effects department as well as dressing-rooms, green room, etc. A canopy—sometimes called 'the heavens'—projected from the tiring-house wall to about half the depth of the stage, and was supported at its outer end on two pillars. There was also a 'machine'—a winch of some kind—by means of which characters or properties could be lowered to the stage from 'the heavens', and trap doors in the floor of the stage through which entry could be made from below. This is a general account, deduced from the evidence of the plays and surviving documents. It is probable that theatres built over a period of about half a century from 1576 had the same general features but differed from each other in detail.

It seems likely that the models that led to the design of the Theatre when James Burbage and his partner John Brayne built it in 1576 were the inn-yard and the bear- or bull-ring. There is evidence that travelling companies of actors had been performing in inn-yards for at least a century before Shakespeare's day. The traditional design of an inn (such as that which is the setting for Scene 1 of Act II of *Henry IV*) was an enclosed yard entered by a gateway from the road, with rooms around it which were occupied by the people staying in the inn. It might be two or three storeys high, and in such cases there was often an open gallery running along the inner side of the yard to give access to the rooms. Several buildings of this style still survive in various parts of England. The company of players could set up a temporary stage against one wall of this yard—and use a room behind for the 'tiring-house'—and control access and collect money at the gate of the yard.

Bull- and bear-baiting—unacceptable sports to modern sensibilities—were popular in sixteenth-century England. A bear or bull was chained in the centre of the ring, and then dogs were set on it. The 'sport' was in the fight which followed. Some dogs were likely to be killed or injured in the process, but the bear was the eventual loser, though the dogs might be called off after a time to allow him to survive, recuperate and fight again another day. Some bears were quite famous: there are a good many references in the period to one called Harry Hunkes. The circular shape of the arena was probably originally defined by the length of the bear's chain, but its advantage in providing the best view for the largest number of people is clear. The addition of galleries for more spectators is

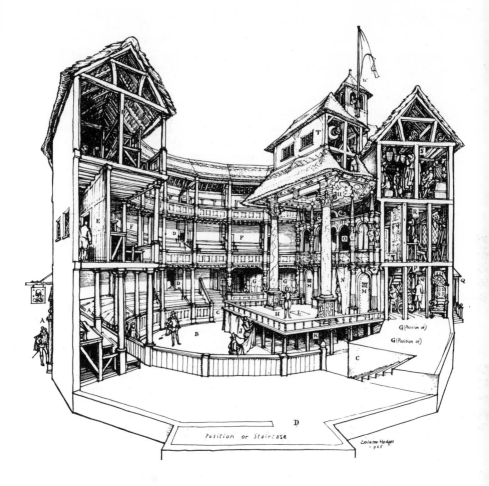

A CONJECTURAL RECONSTRUCTION OF THE INTERIOR OF THE GLOBE PLAYHOUSE

- AA Main entrance
- B The Yard
- CC Entrances to lowest gallery
- D Entrance to staircase and upper galleries
- E Corridor serving the different sections of the middle gallery
- F Middle gallery ('Twopenny Rooms')
- G 'Gentlemen's Rooms' or Lords' Rooms'
- H The stage
- J The hanging being put up round the stage
- K The 'Hell' under the stage
- L The stage trap, leading down to the Hell
- MM Stage doors

- N Curtained 'place behind the stage'
- O Gallery above the stage, used as required sometimes by musicians, sometimes by spectators, and often as part of the play
- P Back-stage area (the tiring-house)
- Q Tiring-house door
- R Dressing-rooms
- S Wardrobe and storage
- T The hut housing the machine for lowering enthroned gods, etc., to the stage
- U The 'Heavens'
- W Hoisting the playhouse flag

a natural development, and then there is something very similar to the Elizabethan theatre building. At least one theatre in London at this time is known to have alternated plays and bear-baiting. It probably had a portable stage that was put up when there were plays, and dismantled and put away on bear-baiting days.

The Elizabethan stage was not a stage of illusions. Plays were presented under natural light on a bare stage which could not be concealed from the audience, and from which all properties had to be removed as soon as they ceased to be relevant to the action. *1 Henry IV* opens with a formal council scene which would require chairs, a throne for the King and probably a council table. All this must be removed for the scene which follows, between the Prince and Falstaff, but similar setting is required again for I.3, the meeting of the Council at Windsor where Hotspur, Northumberland and Worcester are also present. Furniture of a quite different kind would need to be brought on and removed for the tavern scene, II.4. In the same way after battle scenes bodies had to be removed from the stage: so Falstaff removes Hotspur's body at the end of the play. It is not clear, though, how Sir Walter Blunt is removed from the stage after Douglas has killed him—perhaps by minor players dressed as soldiers for the battle. Although the stage presented no scenic illusions, but remained clearly the same through all the changes of the action, it should not be thought of as drab or lacking in spectacle. Costumes were elaborate and expensive, though they did not attempt historical realism: the court of King Henry IV would have worn the costume of Elizabethan gentlemen, a fashion two hundred years after their historical time. Court scenes and battle scenes would have been presented with all possible ceremony and spectacle. The opening stage direction for Act I Scene 3 reads 'Enter the King, Northumberland, Worcester, Hotspur, Sir Walter Blunt, with others'—and this, though many stage directions are not, is from the version of the play printed in Shakespeare's own lifetime. That 'with others' no doubt implies other elaborately dressed councillors who do not have speaking parts, but react appropriately to the abrupt expulsion of Worcester, to Hotspur's account of the battle, and so on. There would also, as this is a formal meeting of the Royal Council, be attendants to bring on and remove the formal insignia, secretaries, messengers, perhaps armed guards at the door. In the same way in battle scenes, or in the scenes of parley before the battle, there would be far more people on stage than those who have speaking parts; trumpeters, standard-bearers and common soldiers. A revealing direction sometimes found for scenes like this in plays of the period is 'as many as may be', implying that every possible member of the company would be brought on to swell a crowd scene or make a battle more impressive. These 'extras' would be used to remove properties (or corpses) at the end of a scene, so that the sequence, the transition from one scene to the next, would be rapid. Roughly, an empty stage indicates the end of a scene and usually a transition to another location.

Most of the editions of Shakespeare's plays that are used today will head each fresh scene with an indication of a location—for instance, Act II, Scene 1 [Rochester. An inn yard]. This is the style used in the Arden Edition and these notes. Such locations are almost always the insertion of later editors of the plays: they are not found in the earliest editions. In I.2.125, in setting out the plan for the robbery, Poins says 'Gadshill lies tonight in Rochester'. It was that which provided the editor (in this case Edward Capell, in the eighteenth century) with the information needed for his scene heading for II.1. Generally, if we need to know precisely the location of a scene, it is told us in the first few lines. In IV.2 we learn at once that Falstaff with his soldiers is in the middle of England, on his way to Shrewsbury: 'Bardolph, get thee before to Coventry'. When IV.4 opens the first person to come on the stage is the Archbishop of York, and he was no doubt dressed in a way that made his ecclesiastical office apparent. Worcester's reference to him at I.3.264 may not be exactly remembered, but the scene serves to remind us that there are other rebels to be dealt with besides those gathered at Shrewsbury, and at the same time it tells us that some supporters of the Percy party are already having misgivings. This scene is also one of the main links with *2 Henry IV* since it is in that play that the Archbishop and Northumberland are tricked into disbanding their army and captured by John of Lancaster. In most cases, of course, where the characters are is sufficiently clear from who they are and what they are doing. If the King is in formal council, the scene is in a council chamber; if the Prince has just been talking to 'a leash of drawers' among 'fourscore hogsheads' then he is in a tavern; if there are soldiers in armour around, then it is probably a battlefield.

Because it did not involve elaborate scenic representation and because properties were always removed when their use on stage was ended, the pace of the action of these plays could be very rapid; scene could flow into scene without breaks or delay. Falstaff and Prince Hal were probably on stage in I.2 almost before the last of the attendants who accompanied the opening scene of the play had left the stage, and while the comments on the Prince's behaviour and the King's unfavourable comparison of him with Hotspur were still fresh in the audience's ears. This rapid flow and significant juxtaposition of parts of the action is not always easy to achieve in the modern theatre, simply because of its much greater technical sophistication and the expectations of the audience that a 'scene' will be presented before them. Another point that must be remembered is the intimacy of the Elizabethan theatre. The most distant spectator could be no more than thirteen metres—thirteen paces—from the stage, and most would be much closer. Favoured persons, it is clear, sometimes sat on the stage itself. All this allowed for rapidity in dialogue and action and a very strong relationship between the players and the audience. There can be little doubt that Falstaff was played by Will Kemp: he was a leading member of the company and a famous clown. When he left the Chamberlain's Men shortly after *1 Henry IV* was written Robert Armin took over as the main comic actor in the company, and Shakespeare (who was writing with particular actors always in mind) produced very different leading comic parts. It is likely then that Falstaff's first appearance would have been greeted with applause from an audience who recognised Kemp, and that Kemp would have responded appropriately. Just as the stage remained the stage while presenting dramatic spectacles, so the actors, too, to a greater degree than in the modern theatre, remained themselves even while presenting dramatic characters, and had a kind of personal intimacy with the audience. This may perhaps still be found in revue or in burlesque in America, or in what is left of the music-hall tradition in England; but it is rarely found any longer in the legitimate theatre.

The Elizabethan world picture

The Renaissance came late to England. That outburst of learning, thought, art and industry that came with the development of a radically new view of human nature marked the change from the medieval to the modern world, from feudalism to capitalism, from loyalty to a lord to patriotism for a nation. There seems a beginning at the magnificent court of Richard II. Geoffrey Chaucer (1340–1400) was his poet, and Chaucer brought into England a knowledge of the new poetry being written in Italy and France. But Richard was deposed and murdered and for most of the next century England was involved either in civil wars or in wars in France. Stable government was finally re-established by Henry VII, and under him and his son Henry VIII learning and the arts began to flourish once more. Erasmus (1466–1534), the great humanist scholar, came to London to converse with Sir Thomas More (1478–1535); Hans Holbein (1497–1543) was the court painter; Cardinal Wolsey (c. 1475–1530) built the great palace at Hampton Court and King Henry completed the wonderful chapel at King's College, Cambridge, that had been begun by the unhappy Henry VI a century before. Sir Thomas Wyatt (1503–42) and the Earl of Surrey (1517?–47) made English again the sonnets of Italy and wrote love poetry that has a distinctively modern voice. But the court of Henry VIII was dangerous as well as magnificent. Wolsey fell; Sir Thomas More was executed; Surrey was beheaded at the age of thirty on a charge of high treason—though his fault was probably little more than irresponsible vanity. Wyatt died a natural death, but he had twice been in the Tower of

London, in danger of the King's anger. Wyatt was perhaps a previous lover of Anne Boleyn, Henry VIII's second wife, Queen Elizabeth I's mother, who was executed on charges of adultery and incest in 1536 after three years' marriage. The separation of England from the Roman Catholic Church, the return under Mary and the renewed break with Elizabeth; the doubts about the succession of Henry VIII's children because of his many marriages and the claims of other grandchildren of Henry VII, Lady Jane Grey and Mary Queen of Scots; these and other factors made the sixteenth century in England a period of doubt and instability, until after 1558 when Queen Elizabeth's good government and great political skill made her secure in the affections of her people, in spite of excommunication by the Pope and bitter hostility from Spain. The great event that marks this rise of national consciousness and pride is the defeat, in 1588, of the Spanish fleet, the Armada. By this victory England defeated the greatest and the wealthiest power in Europe. By that date the great age had already begun. Sir Philip Sidney (1554–86), the ideal courtier, soldier, scholar and poet, had been dead for two years. The 'high astounding terms' of Marlowe's *Tamburlane* had been heard on the English stage in 1587. Edmund Spenser (?1552–99) had been at work on *The Faerie Queene* for several years, and the first three books were published in 1589. It was not only literature which flourished; English music, particularly vocal music, was the finest in Europe, endowed with composers such as William Byrd (1543–1623), John Dowland (1563–1626), Orlando Gibbons (1583–1625) and many others. Painting—particularly of portraits and miniatures—and architecture were also strong. There was a tremendous output of translations. The 'Authorised Version' of the Bible, produced by a committee in the reign of King James I, built on the work of predecessors. While Spenser set out to provide English with its own epic poem in *The Faerie Queene* and to 'overgo Ariosto', the great Italian epic *Orlando Furioso* by Ludovico Ariosto (1474–1533) was translated by Sir John Harington. The *Iliad* and *Odyssey* of Homer were translated into English verse by George Chapman (*c*.1559–1634).

It was not only the arts which flourished, but all kinds of intellectual endeavour—and distinctions which we make between science and art and technology and superstition would have had no meaning for the Elizabethans. John Dee (1527–1608), who was Queen Elizabeth's fortune-teller, was also a brilliant mathematician and a proponent of the Copernican system of astronomy before Galileo (1564–1642), the great Italian astronomer whose observations first demonstrated that the Sun and not the Earth was the centre of our universe. William Gilbert (1540–1603), her doctor, wrote one of the first scientific treatises in *De Magnete* (1600). Francis Bacon (1561–1626), active politician, lawyer and servant of the crown, was also a man of letters and provided the philosophical basis for the empiricism that produced the scientific revolution of another generation. Sir Walter Raleigh (1552–1618), courtier and adventurer, founded the first English colony in America, wrote poems of great power and—imprisoned in the Tower by James I—a magnificent *History of the World* (1614). Journeys of exploration, trade and in many cases simple piracy were financed by the nobility and the great merchant companies of London; Richard Hakluyt (1552–1616) devoted his life to the collection and publication of accounts of voyages and so did much to encourage English exploration and colonisation.

But though England's power, wealth and importance increased enormously, though the Queen and her Council provided good and stable government, and though she was loved and revered by her subjects, we should not accept too rosy a picture of the life of that time. In a period of rapid and radical economic, social and intellectual change the efforts of government were mostly conservative; like most governments at all times they usually applied yesterday's solutions to tomorrow's problems. Unemployment was common, particularly in rural areas. There was a congestion of the cities, particularly London, by the dispossessed, and squalid suburbs developed. Plague was common: in 1564, the year of Shakespeare's birth, more than two hundred and fifty people died from it in the little town of Stratford alone. Though the Queen was enlightened as despots go, she was certainly no democrat and maintained an efficient secret service under Sir Francis Walsingham (c.1530–90). The use of torture was a normal judicial procedure; public executions were common, and these were sometimes, as in the case of Doctor Lopez in 1594 (who was alleged to have attempted to poison the Queen), or 'underground' Jesuits such as Robert Southwell (1561–95), of horrible and spectacular beastliness.

In 1611 the poet and divine John Donne (1573–1631) wrote in 'The First Anniversary':

> The new Philosophy calls all in doubt,
> The Element of fire is quite put out;
> The Sun is lost, and th'earth, and no man's wit
> Can well direct him where to look for it.

This is a familiar passage, and although its immediate reference is to the sensational impact of Galileo's observations and writings on the astronomy of the period, it is used as a typical example of a much more general phenomenon. Galileo declared that the earth was not the centre of the universe, but simply one of a number of planets revolving round a central sun. Under pressure from the Inquisition—the office of the Catholic Church devoted to the detection and eradication of heresy—he later retracted this theory. It is said that as he signed the recantation he whispered to a friend *'E pur si muove!'* (All the same, it [the world] does move!) This idea had been put forward in the previous century by the Polish astronomer Copernicus (1473–1543), but with a significant difference. Copernicus pointed out that with this hypothesis the mathematics of astronomy was very much simplified. Galileo claimed, having observed the transit of the moons of Jupiter, that the Copernican hypothesis was *true*, and could be observed to be true.

The philosophers of the middle ages had elaborated a system of the the world which was orderly, harmonious and self-consistent. For more than a century this system had been under attack, partly because of the new learning of the Renaissance, partly because social and historical change in the world had made the real world and the world of the system increasingly discrepant. The system provided a framework, a hierarchy, a set of relationships and parallels, on which language could continue to draw for analogy, metaphor and symbol at the same time as the system itself was increasingly a matter of debate. This system provides 'the Elizabethan world picture': it is not that everyone accepted and believed the system—such a view would be clearly false—but that the system, representing traditional orthodoxy, was incorporated into the habits of language and thought, even of those who consciously questioned or rejected it. After all we still speak of 'sunrise' and 'sunset', and make frequent metaphorical use of these expressions, although we know that the sun does not rise: the effect is produced by the revolution of the earth. Far more than we realise, perhaps, relics of older ways of thinking are preserved in our language.

An essential part of this system is 'the great chain of being': essentially, everything that exists is in an ordered relation to everything else, from God at the summit down to the lowliest form of matter. There are no gaps in the chain, but everything has an immediate inferior and an immediate superior; at the same time there are correspondences between different sections of the chain. As God is the Lord of all and the sun the chief of the heavenly bodies, so the king is godlike in the political sphere, the lion is the king of beasts or the rose the royal flower. Between these different sections there are linking items. This is clear in the poem 'Providence' by the Anglican divine George Herbert (1593–1623):

Frogs marry fish and flesh; bats, bird and beast;
Sponges, non-sense and sense; mines, th'earth and plants.

Sponges mark the transition between plants and animals and minerals ('mines'), which were thought to grow very slowly within the earth, the link between living and non-living matter. The most important of these links was man, for he came between the beasts and the angels, between the creatures of 'sense' and the creatures of 'intelligence'. Moreover man was a fallen creature, he had broken the chain. Man alone could change his situation, and by God's grace regain his true position.

The material world was composed of the 'four elements', and these provide a basis for the physics, physiology and psychology of the day. The 'elements' are the differing manifestations of the qualities of heat and cold and wetness and dryness. They are Earth, Water, Air and Fire in ascending order: earth and water sink down, air and fire rise up. These were related to the 'four humours' thought of as bodily fluids, which gave rise to both a person's physical and psychological make-up: his 'temperament'. The relations can be schematised thus:

Earth	*dry/cold*	*melancholy*
Water	*cold/wet*	*phlegmatic humour*
Air	*wet/hot*	*sanguine humour (blood)*
Fire	*hot/dry*	*choleric humour*

It will be noted that although the order is ascending from Earth to Fire, it is also circular, since these two elements have, like all the other pairs in the sequence, a common quality; in their case dryness. Since the elements in a substance or the humours in a person were capable of infinite gradation, each along its particular continuum, there was plenty of scope for variety. The ideal was a perfect balance of the humours, for physical and psychological health, but types of the dominance of one humour were characterised. So, for instance, the sanguine humour is courageous, optimistic and amorous. These concepts underlie many of the implications of the language of Shakespeare's plays. The reverberations of an image or metaphor are often a good deal more powerful than the modern use of the same words would suggest.

The sense of national identity, the active patriotism that was felt in England in the later part of the sixteenth century, produced a great interest in history, especially in English history. Many chronicles, annals and similar compilations were made and published at this time, as well as studies of more limited and particular periods. Between 1590 and 1599 Shakespeare wrote nine plays on subjects drawn from English history, and there were numerous other plays by other authors. Samuel Daniel (1562–1619) published a long poem on England's *Civil Wars* in 1595, and Michael Drayton (1563–1631) published a poem on a similar subject, *The Barons' Wars*, in 1603. The main interest in all these cases is in the period of history that preceded the establishment of the Tudor dynasty, and this is not accidental. Among the scholars who came to the court of Henry VII was an Italian, Polydore Vergil (?1470–?1558), who wrote a Latin History of England which, among other things, justified the Tudor establishment. The view of the history of the fifteenth century in England which became almost official policy (and which is sometimes referred to as 'the Tudor myth') was given its fullest form by Edward

Hall (d.1547) in *The Chronicle of the Vnion of the Two Noble and Illustre Families of Lancaster and York*, first published in 1542. Put very crudely, this proposed that the disasters of the Wars of the Roses were a divine judgement and punishment of England for the crime of the deposition and murder of the legitimate king, Richard II, by his cousin, Henry Bolingbroke, who became King Henry IV. In spite of the temporary successes of Henry V's wars in France, the penalty of this crime was the loss of English dominion in France under Henry VI, and a period of bitter civil war, at the end of which Richard III, after a career of intrigue, villainy and murder, came to the throne. His final crime was his murder of his nephews and wards, the 'Princes in the Tower' who were the heirs of Richard's elder brother, who had reigned as Edward IV. God's vengeance struck down Richard at the battle of Bosworth Field in 1485, and His agent was Henry Tudor, Duke of Richmond, who restored legitimate rule and made it more secure by marriage with Elizabeth, the surviving child of Edward IV. This account of recent history as the operation of God's purpose was part of the Elizabethan world picture, and it strongly emphasised the divinely authorised nature of kingship, and the wickedness of any act of rebellion against existing institutions. But just as Copernicus and later Galileo undermined the established views on astronomy, there were radical counter-views of the nature of political power. The spokesman for these was an Italian, Niccolo Machiavelli (1464–1527), and his book *The Prince* (1513) was a very pragmatic essay on statecraft. It was not translated into English before 1640, but it was widely known and misrepresented as devilish wickedness. All the same its recognition that a ruler might have an obligation to act deceitfully, or even perform acts of injustice against particular individuals in order to maintain the good of the whole state was well understood. It was certainly understood in practice by all the Tudor monarchs, not least by Elizabeth herself, however much at variance this may have been with the pieties of the 'Tudor myth'.

Sources

It is clear from his picking-up of particular words and phrases and from his reproduction of errors and confusions that Shakespeare's source for *1 Henry IV* (as for the other history plays, in the main) was *The Chronicles of England* by Raphael Holinshed (?1520–1580), and that he used the second edition of 1587. It is more than likely that he kept it on his work-table and referred to it from time to time as he was writing. Though Shakespeare foreshortens and adjusts for the benefit of his dramatic form, the 'plot' of his history is essentially Holinshed's, and he follows Holinshed in confusing two separate Edmund Mortimers and making them one person (see the note to I.3.144) and in other minor confusions. Indications for some of his characters are also clearly present in the chronicle—the King's policy, his energetic response to the threat of rebellion, his distress at his son's apparent wildness, and his uneasy conscience, are all there, for example. The Prince is given a much more complex character and motivation than appears in Holinshed, and Hotspur's engaging enthusiasm and energy emerge from a few references to his military success and courage in the chronicle. Other characters again—Falstaff, Lady Percy—are almost entirely Shakespeare's invention.

Another account of the events that was clearly well known to Shakespeare was Samuel Daniel's narrative poem published in 1595, *The First Fowre Bookes of the Civile Wars Between the Two Houses of Lancaster and Yorke.* This provided a clear narrative of the events of this play in some thirty stanzas from the third book. Shakespeare follows Daniel in keeping Glendower away from the battle of Shrewsbury: in Holinshed the Welsh were there. Daniel also anticipates Shakespeare in the suggestion of the parallel between Prince Henry and Hotspur as young warriors, though he is less explicit. Like Shakespeare he follows Holinshed in confusing and combining the two Edmund Mortimers.

The anecdotes about the wild youth of Prince Henry are widely dispersed and can be traced back almost to Henry V's own time. Many of those that Shakespeare used are reported by Holinshed, but the immediate source of a good deal of the comic action of *1 Henry IV* can be found in the anonymous play *The Famous Victories of Henry V.* This had been performed as early as 1586, though no edition survives earlier than 1598, when it was probably brought out in the hope of cashing in on the success of Shakespeare's *Henry IV* plays. Here is the original of Sir John Oldcastle/Falstaff and another character, 'Ned', who may be the embryo Poins. There is a highway robbery, and a play-acting scene, and much else. However the chief thing to be learned from a comparison is what genius can make of the most unpromising material, for *The Famous Victories* is crude, confused and incoherent, and its humour is of the coarsest farcical sort.

The moral scheme of the Tudor myth, which saw in history the operation of divine justice, punishing, often in a later generation, the misdeeds of tyrants and usurpers, finds expression in Edward Hall's *Chronicle* (see pp.20–1). This work was well known to the Elizabethans and very widely influenced their thinking about history. Sir Walter Raleigh, for example, in the Preface to his *History of the World* (1614), gives a brief account of the misfortunes of England from the reign of Henry I onwards that is very much in these terms. Hall's providential history may have influenced Shakespeare when he began his great epic scheme of eight plays on English history, but by the time he came to write the second tetralogy he was becoming increasingly doubtful of its validity. It is possible that he referred to Hall during the writing of *1 Henry IV*, but there is no strong evidence that he did.

A note on the text

1 Henry IV was first printed in 1598. Of the earliest edition only four leaves of a single copy survive. However the play was printed again in the same year. So far as can be discovered, this second edition (usually called Quarto 1) was set up from a copy of the earlier one (Q0—Quarto zero). The terms 'quarto' and 'folio' refer to the size of page on which the play is printed, or more precisely, to the number of foldings of a standard size sheet of paper to produce the pages. In a folio the sheet is folded once, to produce two leaves and four pages; in a quarto it is folded twice, to provide four leaves and eight pages. *1 Henry IV* was reprinted more frequently than any other play by Shakespeare in his own lifetime. There were four more quartos before his death: Q2 (1599), Q3 (1604), Q4 (1608) and Q5 (1613). Q6 was published in 1622, the year before the first collected edition of Shakespeare's plays in the 'First Folio' of 1623. It has been established that every one of these editions, including the folio, was set up from one of the earlier printed versions, and that the differences between them are only such as might be produced by accidental error, or by a compositor attempting to correct what was, or what he took to be, error in the copy before him. The essential source, then, for the text of the play is Q1 and the four surviving leaves of Q0 which preceded it. Certain character portrayals in the play raised objections from powerful people after it was performed but before it was printed, and this led to the changing of the names of some characters. It may also have led to some changes in the text of the play itself, but of this we have no evidence. There is evidence, though, in the Q1 text not only that Oldcastle was changed to Falstaff but also that the original names of Bardolph and Peto were Harvey and Sir John Russell. The names survive here and there in speech-headings and stage-directions in both *1 Henry IV* and *2 Henry IV*. Russell was (and still is) the family name of the Earls (now Dukes) of Bedford, and the step-father of the Earl of Southampton (to whom Shakespeare had dedicated his two long poems in 1593 and 1594) was a Harvey. The changes were perhaps wise, even if no direct connection had been made with the forebears of these illustrious families.

The survival of these uncorrected names shows that the printed text was set up from a manuscript in which these names had only been partly corrected: the surviving examples were no doubt oversights of the corrector. It does not appear that this manuscript was one used in the theatre itself, for the Q1 version of the play is rather deficient in stage-directions and other indications that a stage manager is obliged to mark on his script. The usual assumption is that the manuscript that lies behind the early printed versions of the play was probably Shakespeare's own original draft, his 'foul papers' as they were called. From these a careful transcript would have been made for use in the theatre, regularising speech-headings, inserting directions for entries and exits, properties and effects, and marking cuts if the acting-time of the play needed to be reduced.

The text used in the preparation of these notes is the New Arden Edition, ed. A.R. Humphreys, Methuen, London, 1960. All line and scene references in the notes refer to that edition.

Part 2

Summaries
of HENRY IV PART 1

A general summary

The historical events covered in this play are those of about a year, from the capture of Mortimer by Glendower on 22 June 1402 to the defeat of the rebels at the battle of Shrewsbury on 21 July 1403. No clear indications of the passage of time are given in the play and there is some freedom of treatment for dramatic effect. Hotspur's defeat of Douglas at 'Holmedon' took place on 14 September, nearly three months after the battle in Wales though news of both is brought simultaneously to Henry IV in Act I, Scene 1. On the whole, though, Shakespeare follows the events of history—as they were known to the Elizabethans—reasonably closely in this play. Interwoven with the political events are more private ones, concerning the doings of the Prince of Wales with his low companions and his estrangement from, and reconciliation with, his father the King. These events too have a basis of some kind in history and a wide dissemination in popular story, but Shakespeare treats them with considerable freedom and adapts them to his needs. The characters involved in these episodes are essentially the creations of his imagination; and the most famous of them—Sir John Falstaff—is explicitly denied resemblance to a particular historical character: 'for Oldcastle died martyr, and this is not the man' (*2 Henry IV*, epilogue). Falstaff was originally called Oldcastle (see the note to I.2.41, where the Prince calls Falstaff 'my old lad of the castle') but the name was changed before the play was printed.

Perhaps the most interesting change Shakespeare makes to history is to adjust the relative ages of some of the characters. In *Richard II* Henry Bolingbroke appears a comparatively young man, contrasted with an older generation represented by his father, John of Gaunt, and his uncle, the Duke of York. In *1 Henry IV*, although its events follow, within a couple of years, the murder of Richard II, King Henry seems already an old man, and, along with Westmoreland, Worcester and Northumberland, is contrasted with a younger generation represented by Prince Henry, Hotspur and Mortimer. In particular it is implied that Hotspur and Prince Henry are the same age:

O that it could be prov'd
That some night-tripping fairy had exchang'd

In cradle-clothes our children where they lay,
And call'd mine Percy, his Plantagenet!

(I.1.85–8)

In fact, Hotspur was born in 1364, and was three years older than Henry IV himself. Prince Hal was born in 1387. There is no way of telling whether Shakespeare knew that he was changing people's ages but it is easy to see the advantages to the dramatist in making neat contrasts between parties and generations. In particular the opposition between Prince Henry and Hotspur which ends with their combat at the battle of Shrewsbury is much more effective if they are seen as more or less equal in age and experience.

The main political action of the play concerns the rebellion of the Percys against Henry IV, whose cause they had originally supported. At the opening of the play they are still playing their family's traditional role as guardians of the border with Scotland. A state of endemic warfare and border raiding continued until the union of England and Scotland with the accession of James I. When Hotspur is provoked by the King's refusal to ransom Mortimer, and his demand for Hotspur's prisoners, Worcester and Northumberland, Hotspur's uncle and father, initiate him into the plot they have already laid to raise a rebellion and remove King Henry IV from the throne. It might appear in this scene that the rebellion is to be in favour of Mortimer, the legitimate heir to Richard II, but when we do meet Mortimer with Glendower in III.1. we learn that England is to be divided into three. The price Mortimer is to pay is an independent Wales, enlarged by those English counties (the Welsh Marches) west of the River Severn, while the Percys are to get a new independent kingdom of their own north of the Trent. The chronicles also list concessions to be made to Douglas, but these are not mentioned in the play. For the Elizabethans, this plan removed any shadow of legitimacy from the rebellion, for to divide the kingdom was a serious crime, likely to produce (as in *King Lear* or the early tragedy *Gorboduc*) terrible consequences and further civil war. The implications of this are already present in Hotspur's irresponsible cavilling:

Methinks my moiety, north from Burton here,
In quantity equals not one of yours:
See how this river comes me cranking in . . .

(III.1.92–4)

And then, when Glendower agrees to 'have Trent turned', he replies: 'I do not care, I'll give thrice so much land/To any well-deserving friend' (131–2).

If Hotspur is irresponsible in this and in his deliberate provocation of Glendower in the same scene, the other conspirators show a different kind of irresponsibility later on. King Henry and his supporters take rapid and effective action against the rebels, and are prepared for battle before they are expected. Both Glendower and Northumberland of the other party fail to bring their armies to the battle, and Mortimer is not heard of again. Hotspur, Worcester and Douglas are left to fight a considerably larger royal army at the battle of Shrewsbury. Hotspur is killed by Prince Henry in the battle; Douglas is captured and, by a chivalric gesture of Prince Henry's, set free; Worcester is sent to execution. The play ends with this victory, but the rebellion is not over and the last speeches look forward to *2 Henry IV* which completes the Lancastrian success and ends with the death of Henry IV and the coronation of Henry V.

Interwoven with the political action of the Percy rebellion are the scenes involving Falstaff and the other low-life characters. The relation of these is episodic: there is no single line of action running through them. On the other hand they are a good deal more than 'comic relief', and the juxtaposition with the political scenes often makes an oblique comment. We first see Prince Hal just after his father has made his unfavourable comparison with Hotspur, and the first impression is to confirm this gloomy view. We see the Prince joking coarsely—if cleverly—with low persons, and plotting a highway robbery only a little mitigated by the practical joke by some of the robbers upon the others that is also planned. There are, however, qualifications to be made to this view. The first is the direction of much of the Prince's innuendo; it can be illustrated in this passage:

FALSTAFF: Do not thou when thou art king hang a thief.
PRINCE: No, thou shalt.
FALSTAFF: Shall I? O rare! By the lord, I'll be a brave judge!
PRINCE: Thou judgest false already, I mean thou shalt have the hanging of the thieves, and so become a rare hangman.
(I.2.59–65)

A third interpretation, that Falstaff will be hanged for a thief when Henry is king, is plain enough. The sardonic and bitter edge that is to be found in the Prince's wit from the first implies an element of self-disgust at his own behaviour and a certain callousness in his disposition. It prepares us emotionally for the soliloquy which ends the scene, in which the Prince announces his intention to reform and makes clear that his traditional 'wildness' is a matter of calculation and conscious choice.

The introduction of the Prince is followed by the first appearance of Hotspur, and the proposal of the Gad's Hill robbery is followed by the proposal of the rebellion. The two scenes showing the robbery follow and then a short scene between Hotspur and his wife provides the interval before the great tavern scene which is the aftermath of the robbery. After some preliminary teasing of a witless potboy the exposure of Falstaff's cowardice is developed—the comic situation for which Poins's joke of robbing the robbers was proposed. Falstaff turns the joke back on the Prince and Poins when he claims to have known all along what was happening:

> By the Lord, I knew ye as well as he that made ye. Why, hear you, my masters, was it for me to kill the heir-apparent? Should I turn upon the true prince?
>
> (II.4.263–5)

The grossness of the exaggerations of his previous account supports his claim. The comedy then turns to a parody of an important event to follow, the reconciliation of the Prince with his father. First the Prince plays himself and Falstaff his father, and then the roles are reversed: this provides a further occasion for the exercise of Hal's black sense of humour at Falstaff's expense:

> FALSTAFF: [as the Prince]—but for sweet Jack Falstaff, kind Jack Falstaff, true Jack Falstaff, valiant Jack Falstaff, and therefore more valiant, being as he is old Jack Falstaff, banish not him thy Harry's company, banish not him thy Harry's company, banish plump Jack, and banish all the world.
> PRINCE: [as the King] I do, I will.   (II.4.469–75)

And, of course, at the end of *2 Henry IV*, he does. At this point the extempore play is interrupted by the arrival of a hue and cry at the door of the inn in pursuit of Falstaff for the Gad's Hill robbery. Falstaff is hidden, the Sheriff outfaced by the Prince, and the scene ends with the assurance that the money will be paid back again 'with advantage'.

The celebration of the ill-gotten gains of Gad's Hill is directly followed by the scene in which the rebels propose the division of the kingdom, and that by the event we have seen parodied shortly before, the interview between King Henry IV and his son. There is one more Eastcheap scene, in which, as all the action begins to focus on the battle to come, Falstaff is provided with a command of foot soldiers, and the Prince is cheerful and briskly efficient.

In the first scene of Act IV news is brought to Hotspur, Douglas and Worcester that Northumberland is sick, and unable to bring his army to meet them at Shrewsbury. Sir Richard Vernon arrives with the news that powerful royal armies are approaching, and then, in response to a caustic enquiry from Hotspur, launches into a eulogy of Prince Henry. The scene ends with the information that Glendower, too, will not arrive with his forces to support them in the imminent battle. The brief scene with Falstaff on the march to Shrewsbury with his troops allows him to admit in soliloquy 'I have misused the King's press damnably' (IV.2.12), and so to comment, by implication, on the abuses of the Queen's 'press' (the power to conscript soldiers for the royal army in times of need) still current in the end of the sixteenth century.

In the rebel camp the night before the battle, Hotspur and Douglas argue for an immediate attack while Worcester and Vernon propose delay. Sir Walter Blunt comes as an embassy from the King, to ask the nature of the rebels' grievances and to offer to remedy them. This provokes Hotspur to a vehement restatement of Henry IV's devious path to the throne, but he concludes, with an abrupt change of tone, with the proposal of a further parley 'in the morning early', thereby implicitly accepting the arguments of Vernon and Worcester against an immediate battle.

The Archbishop of York's brief appearance reminds us that, even if the King wins the battle at Shrewsbury, the rebellion is by no means over and it points forward to *2 Henry IV*. It also serves to bridge the time gap between the night parley in the rebel camp and the morning meeting when Worcester comes with Vernon to parley with the King. Worcester and the King go through the expected motions of injured virtue on each side, and then Prince Henry brings in a new proposal with his offer to let the matter be settled by single combat between himself and Hotspur. However, immediately the rebel embassy has departed he says 'It will not be accepted, on my life' (V.1.115), and the royal army prepares for battle. The peace negotiations, in fact, are all too similar to those which are still familiar to us, where the main motive of each side seems to be to justify its own position, where there is no trust of the offers made on either side, and nothing is achieved. The scene ends fittingly with Falstaff's cynical and pragmatic soliloquy on the nature of 'honour'. The point is reinforced when this is at once followed by Worcester persuading Vernon that the King is not to be trusted, and that they are therefore justified in not even reporting his offer, or the Prince's, back to the other rebel leaders.

The battle is engaged, and lost and won, but even here guile is important. Stafford and Sir Walter Blunt are killed by Douglas because they are dressed like the King; Falstaff survives because he knows when 'the better part of valour is discretion' (V.4.119) and plays dead when in danger from Douglas. And finally, though Prince Henry kills Hotspur, Falstaff claims the credit.

Detailed summaries

Act I Scene 1 [London. The palace]*

The play opens with a formal scene of the King in council. His first speech looks forward to an end of civil war and the fulfilment of his ambition to lead a crusade to Jerusalem. But it rapidly becomes clear that this is a dream and not a realistic proposal. The council is to discuss ways and means of dealing with a rebellion in Wales led by Glendower, which has defeated an English army, and captured their commander, Mortimer. Better news is that a Scots army has been defeated by Henry Hotspur, son of the Earl of Northumberland, and important prisoners taken. The King reflects sadly on the comparison between Hotspur's achievements and the disreputable behaviour of his own son Henry. An indication of trouble to come is given in Hotspur's refusal—provoked by Worcester—to hand his prisoners over to the King. The council is concluded, to be re-convened at Windsor on 'Wednesday next'.

NOTES AND GLOSSARY:

So shaken ... dear expedience: the King's ambition to lead a crusade against the Saracens is partly a dream (he is never sufficiently secure for it to be possible), partly an act of penance for his own sin in taking the throne from Richard II and conniving at Richard's murder, and partly a political scheme, to get his unruly nobility involved in fighting and looking for the spoils somewhere else than at home

Mortimer: see below (I.3.79 and 144)

Glendower: 'irregular and wild': in the Chronicles, the leader of a guerrilla army retreating to the mountains when hard pressed. The magician and poet who appears in Act III is Shakespeare's invention

corpse: this form was commonly used for the plural at this time

Upon ... spoken of: Holinshed is as decently reticent as Shakespeare about what 'those Welshwomen' did, but it appears from other reports that they castrated the dead soldiers and put their genitals in their mouths

Here is ... welcome news: it is significant that Henry is better informed than his Council, and makes a point of being so. Compare III.2.172, where Sir Walter Blunt again brings urgent news, and is told it is five days old

*The square brackets throughout indicate that the scene location is not original, but provided by later editors.

Mordake:	the modern spelling of this name is Murdoch
Menteith:	in fact one of Mordake's other titles, not a separate person
The prisoners ... Earl of Fife:	under the 'rules of war' Hotspur was entitled to ransom all his prisoners (except Mordake, who was of royal blood) for his own advantage. It is possible then that Henry IV should be seen as himself provoking the confrontation that follows. However, Hotspur never makes this claim, and the issue is not clear
Worcester:	he is generally reported as malevolent and given to stirring up trouble
prune:	preen
Windsor:	Windsor Castle is still the main residence of the English Royal Family

---

Act I Scene 2 [London. An apartment of the Prince's]

An abrupt and calculated contrast with the previous scene is provided here, from verse to prose, from affairs of state to drinking, eating, sleeping, whoring and stealing. Having just heard that 'riot and dishonour stain the brow' of 'young Harry', we now see the Prince and some of his companions. The Prince's wit is abrasive, Falstaff's more good-humoured, but the impression given is that they are playing a game they have played many times before. Poins enters with the news that Gadshill has 'set a match' (planned a robbery). The Prince at first refuses to be involved, but then, after Falstaff has left, agrees to join Poins in the practical joke of robbing the robbers. The scene closes with a soliloquy (in verse, in contrast to the prose dialogue that has gone before), in which Prince Henry makes clear that his 'loose behaviour' is by no means what it appears on the surface. As a consequence, the audience has a fuller understanding of his actions than is available to any character in the play.

It is clear that Falstaff and Poins are 'gentlemen', though in reduced circumstances. Their manner and speech, and the way the Prince responds to them, distinguish them from Bardolph and Peto, who appear later. Poins, indeed, is 'one it pleases me for fault of a better to call my friend', as the Prince ruefully admits in *2 Henry IV*, II.2.40. All the same, the degree of intimacy is always carefully controlled by the Prince; he closes the interview with Poins briefly and firmly, and Poins's sense of this is marked by his shift from the familiar 'sweet Hal' of his greeting to the formal 'farewell, my lord'. Notable in the earlier part of the scene is Falstaff's repeated stress on 'when thou art king' (ll.16, 23, 58, 141), which indicates his hopes for future advantages. His apparent affection for the young Prince Henry is by no means disinterested.

In the repartee of this scene the jokes are often obscure, depending on complicated puns or allusions to things long forgotten. For a full explanation reference should be made to a well annotated edition of the play (see Part 5, Suggestions for further reading).

NOTES AND GLOSSARY:

Now, Hal ... gallows: the Prince suggests that time is irrelevant to Falstaff, who is governed by his appetites alone. Falstaff picks up 'day' from 'time of the day' and claims that, as a thief, he belongs to night, not day, the moon, not the sun. The Prince accepts this, and again turns the conversation in a direction Falstaff does not like by reference to the ebbs and flows of fortune, and a conclusion at the gallows

And is not ... wench?: Falstaff again changes the subject

old lad of the Castle: the fat knight in *The Famous Victories of Henry V* is Sir John (Jockey) Oldcastle and it is clear that Shakespeare originally used this name. The objection came from Henry Cobham, Earl Brooke, a descendant of the historical Oldcastle. This man had been a friend of Prince Henry (though not a disreputable one) and, being a follower of John Wycliffe (1320–84), a religious reformer anticipating some of the ideas of the Reformation, had been burned at the stake for heresy in the reign of Henry V, in spite of royal attempts to persuade him to change his views. While England remained Catholic it is easy to see why an early Protestant should be presented as a misleader of the young prince. Equally, in Queen Elizabeth's reign, he becomes an early Protestant martyr, and so cannot any longer be disreputable. At the same time, this passage can stand (if not simply overlooked) because a 'lad of the castle' was a term for a roisterer: The Castle was a well-known brothel in Southwark, the same district as the Globe Theatre

buff jerkin: leather coat, worn by constables

durance: imprisonment

Why, what a pox ... tavern?: the Prince rejects Falstaff's attempt to associate him with the hostess in a sexual liaison

here apparent ... heir apparent: a pun. The 'heir apparent' is the obvious successor to the throne

old Father Antic: Falstaff represents the law as a senile buffoon

hang a thief: there are three senses here: (1) judicial: condemn to be hanged, (2) execution: to perform the hanging, as executioner, and (3) to be hanged as a thief. This last is not made explicit

suits: another pun: the clothes of the condemned were one of the perquisites of the hangman. On the other hand, 'waiting in court' might be a way of winning 'suits' in the sense of petitions

gib cat: castrated tom-cat

lugged bear: baited bear

melancholy: here, bad-smelling

Moor-ditch: a narrow and filthy stream in London, then acting as a sewer

comparative: given to making comparisons

wisdom ... regards it: from the Bible, Proverbs 1:20,24

iteration: facility in quotation

baffle: hang up by the feet: a punishment for false knights

Gadshill: the person takes his name from the place, Gad's Hill (see l.121) two miles out of Rochester (see l.125), in Kent, on the London road, about twenty miles from London. It was a notorious haunt of highwaymen

Sack—and Sugar: this is a place where the Quarto text seems to need emendation. 'Sack' was white wine from Spain. The addition of sugar would make it more palatable to a 'sweet tooth', and 'sack and sugar' appears to have been a favourite drink for old people

Good Friday: a day of strict fast

Capon: a de-sexed cockerel

pilgrims ... offerings: destined for the shrine of St Thomas à Becket, the most important site of pilgrimage in England before the Reformation. Becket (1118–70) was the friend and Chancellor of Henry II but after becoming Archbishop of Canterbury in 1162 opposed the King's attempts to reduce the power of the Church. This led to his murder in Canterbury Cathedral. He was seen as a martyr of the Church and made a saint in 1173

vizards: masks

Eastcheap: a street in the eastern part of the old city of London, not far from the Tower

Yedward: a variant of Edward

Chops: 'fat face'

Well, God give ... countenance: Falstaff parodies the language of puritans

All-hallown summer: All Hallows (All Saints) day is 1 November, so this means 'Indian summer', or fine weather out of season. The joke is at Falstaff's combination of age with youthful irresponsibility

How shall ... ?: the Prince's questions of Poins here are brief, and very much to the point. He sums up the plan, and its possible difficulties very quickly: a thoroughly practical young man

noted: conspicuous. Holinshed provides evidence that the Prince had a taste for fancy clothes

I know ... I will: Prince Henry's soliloquy makes use of standard comparisons from the 'great chain of being'. The sun is the 'king' of the planets, and so the sun obscured by clouds is an appropriate image for a royal person mixing in low society. Gold—'bright metal'—is the highest of the metals, and its brightness appears most clearly against a dull, unreflecting background ('a sullen ground')

Act I Scene 3 [Windsor. The council chamber]

The first council scene opened quietly, with the King melancholy and reflective, but also formal in his address to his Council. This one is quite different. The rhyming couplet that concluded the Prince's soliloquy at the end of the previous scene is a firm close. We may assume that there is a brief pause while the stage is set with chairs and council-table, and that the King comes on already in the flow of angry speech. Worcester's unwelcome reminder of past benefits increases the anger, and he is sent out of the room like a naughty boy. It is a very exciting opening to the scene, but it is quite possible to think of it as a calculated display of his authority by the King. When Worcester is gone the King's tone to Northumberland is only marginally milder. Hotspur now appears for the first time, and we are able to make comparisons with the Prince who has just left the stage. There is an attractive vehemence about Hotspur, but it is soon clear, in spite of Sir Walter Blunt's rather clumsy intervention, that neither side to the dispute is prepared to give way.

A new issue is introduced with the mention of Mortimer, but it only makes the dispute more heated. It ends with the King giving commands, and tactically leaving before there is time for them to be refused to his face. Hotspur is left in a rage, and, with the return of Worcester, this is used as an occasion to recapitulate some of the events that went before the opening of the play: the deposition and murder of Richard II. This leads to the introduction (when he has finally quietened down) of Hotspur into the plot to depose Henry IV.

NOTES AND GLOSSARY:

found me: found my good nature, and taken advantage of it

The ... brow: 'the angry defiance of a subject's frown' (*Arden*)

Those prisoners ... my son: Northumberland does not say that Hotspur did not deny the prisoners

My liege ... unsay it now: Hotspur presents himself as a blunt, pragmatic soldier, but—as this energetically satiric portrait of the courtier on the battle-field, and many other speeches show—he has a vivid imagination. (Compare I.3.207: 'He apprehends a world of figures here')

milliner: a dealer in hats, gloves, collars, laces, and other small articles of dress. These, especially gloves, were frequently perfumed

pouncet-box: small box with a 'pounced' (perforated) lid, for sweet-smelling herbs and spices

took it in snuff: sniffed it up. The phrase also means 'got angry about it'. Tobacco snuff was probably being taken in England when the play was written, but the 'snuffing' of aromatic and medicinal powders certainly goes back well before the reign of Henry IV

grief: pain

parmacity: spermaceti

tall: brave

vile guns: although hand-guns were in use in Shakespeare's day, the reference here is probably to heavier pieces. The development of effective artillery made a radical—and lamented—change in the nature of war. In particular, the stone-built castle was not the defence it used to be, and 'guns' were one of the reasons for the strong central governments of the Tudors, and the decline of the feudal barons

Mortimer: two persons are confused here, by Shakespeare, as by his sources, Holinshed and Daniel. The Edmund Mortimer who was defeated by Glendower was the brother of Roger Earl of March (l.83), not himself the earl. Roger had died in 1398, and his son, also Edmund Mortimer, fifth Earl of March, was only a boy at this time, and firmly in the King's power

Marry'd: Roger Mortimer had been Glendower's prisoner, unransomed, for more than three months before this marriage. This is concealed because in I.1. the battles in Wales (June) and Scotland (September) are reported simultaneously

indent: make an agreement
He never ... combatants: there is no independent evidence for this heroic combat
crisp head: here Shakespeare is personifying the river Severn as a god with curly hair (Latin *crispus*: curled), appropriate to the ripples on the surface of flowing water
choler: the hot dry 'humour', an excess of which manifested itself in anger. By this point Hotspur has lost control of himself
ingrate and canker'd: ungrateful and diseased. The reference of 'canker'd' is complex: the canker-worm particularly attacked roses, and so 'cankered' could mean 'rotten inside', 'morally diseased',—and the red rose was the emblem of the House of Lancaster. At the same time a canker is an outward sore or coarse spot on the skin and Henry IV historically suffered from a chronic skin disease, probably psoriasis
my wife's brother ... next of blood: the same confusion as at 1.79: Richard proclaimed Roger, fourth Earl of March, his heir, and following Roger's death, his son Edmund, the nephew of Hotspur's brother-in-law. Hotspur's wife, 'Kate' in the play, 'Elizabeth' in history, was the elder sister of Roger and Edmund
brother: brother-in-law; Hotspur's brother-in-law was, as pointed out above, uncle to the proclaimed heir (compare III.1.190 where Mortimer refers to Hotspur's wife as 'my aunt Percy')
murderous subornation: being accessories to the murder (of Richard II)
line ... predicament: 'the precise charges'—but 'predicament' also carries its modern sense of 'danger'
To put down ... Bolingbroke: in the 'chain of being' the rose is the royal flower; the 'canker' is the unesteemed wild rose
cousin: loosely used of any near relative at this time. Hotspur is Worcester's nephew (compare IV.3.99)
If he fall in ... pot of ale: Hotspur indulges himself in a ranting outburst, and is very properly reprimanded by his father
Scot: plays on the meaning of 'scot', small payment, originally a kind of tax (compare the modern expression 'scot free')
starling: starlings are imitative birds, and easily learn a few words
sword-and-buckler: disorderly person
woman's mood: lack of self-control was thought to be a woman's weakness

pismires:	ants
politician:	almost always a term of abuse at this time. A subtle, crafty and unprincipled person
madcap Duke:	Edmund Langley, Duke of York, is reported to have given more attention to the pleasures of life than its responsibilities
kept:	lived
Ravenspurgh:	on the Yorkshire coast, where Henry Bolingbroke landed on his unauthorised return from exile. The fort has since disappeared under the sea
Berkley Castle:	in Gloucestershire. The meeting Hotspur refers to is presented in *Richard II*, II.3.21–50. Henry was less fulsome than Hotspur suggests
cousin ... cozeners:	to cozen is to cheat, or deceive. The pun is a common one in the period
the Douglas' son:	it is the practice to distinguish the senior member of each of the great Scottish families with the definite article. 'The Douglas' is the leading member of his clan. Shakespeare follows a printer's error in Holinshed in making Mordake, who was heir to the Scottish throne, the son of Douglas
His brother's death:	it was the Archbishop's cousin, not brother, who was executed at Bristol (see *Richard II*, III.2.142)
Before ... slip:	'as usual, you are letting your hounds loose before there is anything for them to pursue'
suddenly:	very soon

Act II Scene 1 [Rochester. An inn yard]

The naturalistic prose of the two carriers is in sharp contrast to Hotspur's heroics and the elevated verse of the previous scene. It adds a dimension to the play by giving us a glimpse of ordinary decent people and their problems. They are clearly suspicious of Gadshill when he enters. The carriers leave, and Gadshill is joined by Chamberlain (this could be either a name or the title of the inn servant in charge of the bedchambers). The two discuss the proposed robbery, indicate that they know important people are likely to be involved, and incidentally offer some social comment.

NOTES AND GLOSSARY:

Charles' wain:	the constellation known as the Plough, or the Great Bear. To tell the time by the stars (four by the day: four a.m.) requires great familiarity, since their positions vary throughout the year

horse: horses. The unchanged plural form was common usage (as 'sheep' still is)

ostler: stable man, groom

I prithee ... all cess: the carriers have pack-horses. 'Cut' would be a horse with a docked tail or (probably) a gelding. The pack-saddle has galled its withers (the top of the shoulders) badly, and the padding in the saddle needs to be softened and shifted, so that it will bear less on the injury

dank as a dog: damp, mouldy

bots: intestinal worms

price of oats: the price increased threefold between 1593 ar d 1596

tench: a small spotted fish

by the mass ... better bit: kings should have the most of everything— including flea-bites, apparently

first cock: midnight

Why, they will ... fleas: 'They don't let us have a chamber pot, so we make water in the fireplace, and stale urine in a room engenders fleas'

loach: a small fresh-water fish

gammon: leg

razes: roots

as far as Charing Cross: on the far side of the city of London from Rochester

pate: head

two o'clock: the carrier is deliberately misleading (compare l.1 when he says it is four a.m.)

soft: 'take it easy'

Time enough ... thee: the carriers refuse to give Gadshill any information

great charge: a lot to take care of: but the strongest implication is of money

At hand, quoth pickpurse: a traditional joke: 'ready to serve you'

thou layest the plot how: you give directions how the job is to be done

Wild: weald: an area of Kent originally forest

auditor: Royal officer who examined accounts

presently: at once

Saint Nicholas' clerks: highway robbers: St. Nicholas—Santa Claus— 'Father Christmas'—was the patron saint of children and travellers. The story of his miraculous intervention to make some robbers restore stolen property was well known. The ironic application of his name to robbers was common. His emblem, three balls (purses) of gold, has become the sign for a pawnbroker

Troyans: Trojans; in this context, drinking-companions

foot land-rakers: vagabonds, tramps

long staff sixpenny strikers: cheap thieves who use a long pole to knock travellers down

malt ... maltworms: maltworms are drinkers (malt is used in brewing beer) who become purple-faced after years of toping. Notice the many jokes in the play about Bardolph's complexion. Large moustaches, taken as a sign of bravery, were affected by old soldiers and 'roarers' generally

burgomasters: originally Dutch, the chief magistrate of a town. Here, jocularly, 'important people'

oneyers: no simple explanation of this word is available. It is possibly a misprint, but the sense is clearly 'people of power and wealth'

pray ... boots: complicated punning on 'pray' and 'prey' and 'boots' in the sense of (1) plunder and (2) footwear

hold ... way: be waterproof on a muddy road

liquored: (1) (of boots) oiled to make waterproof; (2) (of the Commonwealth, personified) made drunk; (3) bribed

fern seed: it was a common belief that a man could be made invisible if he carried fern seed—but as fern seed itself was invisible (except on Midsummer eve) it was hard to obtain

true: a quibble on 'true' in the sense of (1) 'honourable' and (2) 'veritable'

homo: (_Latin_) man

muddy: dull

Act II Scene 2 [Gad's Hill. The highway]

This scene involves the double robbery on Gad's Hill, first of the travellers by Falstaff, Bardolph and Peto, and then of the thieves by Poins and the Prince. The tone throughout is of high-spirited horseplay rather than crime. The travellers make only a very brief appearance, and their only words are pious platitudes.

NOTES AND GLOSSARY:

frets: a pun (1) (of people) worries, gets angry; (2) (of cloth) frays

gummed velvet: velvet was sometimes treated with gum to make it glossy, but velvet so treated 'fretted' (frayed) very easily

squier:	square: a measuring instrument
medicines:	love-potions
thieves ... another:	a comic application of the proverb 'there is honour among thieves'
colt:	trick. A pun on the meaning 'a young horse'
heir-apparent garters:	'hang in your own garters' was a common imprecation. Hal's are 'heir apparent' because, as Prince of Wales, he was a member of the Order of the Garter
peach:	betray; turn king's evidence
ballads made on you all:	the trials of famous criminals (and their executions) were frequently the subject of ballads. Ballad-makers could also be hired to lampoon enemies
jest:	highway robbery is a 'jest' to Falstaff
John of Gaunt:	'gaunt' means emaciated, and Prince Henry, accoding to tradition, was tall and thin (compare the abuse at II.4.240-4)
happy ... dole:	proverb: 'may each of us be a happy man'
caterpillar:	Falstaff projects his own faults on to the travellers. A 'caterpillar' is a social parasite
Got ... pity him:	the Prince indicates the close of the scene and his own authority by shifting from prose to verse

Act II Scene 3 [Warkworth. The castle]

This scene opens with Hotspur alone, reading a letter, the writer of which refuses to join the rebellion. Hotspur is indignant, angry, and in the end talks himself back into over-confidence. Two implications can be drawn: that support for the rebellion is not widespread, and that Hotspur may have been rash in the selection of people to call on for support. Lady Percy—Kate—enters with a long formal speech of complaint about Hotspur's preoccupation and disturbance. He refuses to respond on her level of seriousness, but responds with humorous affection, giving her no information but promising 'Whither I go, thither shall you go too'.

NOTES AND GLOSSARY:

Warkworth Castle:	at this time this was the main residence of the Percy family, and Hotspur is clearly at home in this scene
Kate:	Holinshed calls her 'Elianor' and she was baptised 'Elizabeth'. Why Shakespeare chose 'Kate' (except perhaps that he liked the name) is unknown
stomach:	appetite

thick-eyed:	unobservant, inattentive
curst:	bad-tempered
manage:	horsemanship
basilisks ... culverin:	large and small artillery
hest:	command
roan:	a horse in which hair of two distinct colours (one of them commonly white) is mixed evenly over the body
Esperance:	the Percy motto and battle-cry, meaning 'hope'
weasel ... spleen:	the spleen was thought to be the source of irritable emotions, and weasels were typically bad-tempered and quarrelsome
brother ... title:	Mortimer, her brother, was 'stirring', but (see above I.3.79) he had no title. That rested with his nephew
line:	strengthen
mammets:	dolls
I know you ... gentle Kate:	Hotspur produces a version of an anti-feminist joke that goes back to the elder Seneca at least: it is a nice irony that the letter he was reading when the scene opened indicated that he had told too much, and to the wrong people

---

Act II Scene 4 [Eastcheap. The Boar's Head Tavern]

The Prince has been continuing his education among the lower classes, the inn servants. He has apparently pleased them, but his derisive tone when talking to Poins is as of a different and certainly inferior species. The teasing of Francis follows, and then Falstaff and the others arrive. Falstaff is in a bad humour, and tells an epic story of his valour at Gad's Hill. The Prince and Poins expose his lies, and he—as usual—evades the trap with his assertion (not improbable in any case) that he knew them all the time. It was not for him, as a loyal citizen, to fight against the King's son. A messenger from court comes for the Prince, with news—conveyed by Falstaff—of the coming rebellion. He warns the Prince that he will be 'horribly chid tomorrow' when he sees his father. An extempore rehearsal of that scene is played, first with the Prince playing himself, and Falstaff the King, and then with these roles reversed. There is then a great knocking at the door: the sheriff and the watch have come to search the house for the Gad's Hill robbers. The Prince, with calm authority, satisfies the sheriff, and sends him away. At the end of the scene, Falstaff, who had been hidden behind the wall-hangings, is found fast asleep. His pockets are searched, and the Prince takes the papers found there. He proposes to procure Falstaff 'a charge of foot' in the coming wars.

NOTES AND GLOSSARY:

The Boar's Head Tavern: this is never specifically mentioned by Shakespeare, though at I.2.186–7 the Prince had told Poins he would 'sup' in Eastcheap. The Boar's Head was a famous tavern there in Shakespeare's day, and there are punning allusions to the title in *2 Henry IV*, II.2.159

fat room: either a room where vats were kept or a 'stuffy' room

loggerheads: blockheads

hogsheads: large casks of fifty-two-and-a-half gallons capacity

leash: set of three

Corinthian: good drinking-companion

breathe in your watering: stop for breath before you have emptied a glass

hem: 'clear your throat'

play it off: 'get on with it'

tinker: tinkers were famous drinkers, and had a private language, the 'canting tongue'

underskinker: inferior drawer of wine

Anon: 'at once'

bastard: a sweet Spanish wine

Half-moon: the various rooms in an inn had different names, and a corresponding sign on the door, for the benefit of the illiterate

puny: inexperienced

Pomgarnet: Pomegranate, another room in the inn

serve ... years: Francis has served less than two years of his seven-year apprenticeship

indenture: the contract of apprenticeship

Michaelmas: 29 September

Wilt thou ... pouch: crystal buttons on a leather jerkin were in fashion about twenty years before the play was written; 'not pated' is with hair cropped short; 'puke' stockings were of heavy dark wool; 'caddis-garters' were made of worsted tape; a 'Spanish [leather] pouch' was part of a vintner's equipment. It seems that the Prince is describing Francis's master in a thoroughly confusing manner

Why, then ... so much: this seems complete nonsense

Barbary: sugar was grown in Barbary, the coastal area of North Africa

I am now ... midnight: 'I am in the mood for any fancy that any man has had since the creation of the world'

parcel of a reckoning: items of a bill

work:	real fighting
drench:	dose of medicine
an hour after:	Hotspur's habit of responding to questions after a delay can be observed at II.3.65–91. The Prince's own preoccupations are perhaps indicated by his abrupt change of subject to talk of Hotspur and 'Dame Mortimer his wife'
Rivo:	a common cry among drinkers, of obscure meaning
nether stocks:	stockings
Didst thou ... compound:	an obscure passage that may be corrupt. Presumably Falstaff's round red face is Titan, the sun, that melted a dish of butter as quickly as he swallows a cup of wine
lime:	used to make wine clear
shotten herring:	a (male) herring that has shot its roe in the breeding season
weaver ... psalms:	weavers at this time had a reputation for puritanism and frequently sang religious songs at their work
dagger of lath:	wooden dagger: the equipment of a professional fool
and:	if
at half-sword:	close quarters: the distance of half a sword's length
buckler:	small round shield
ecce signum:	(*Latin*) behold the sign
an Ebrew Jew:	a very Jewish Jew
bunch of radish:	eating radishes was supposed to make people thin
thou ... point:	Falstaff demonstrates his sword technique; 'ward' is a defensive posture; 'point' is a sword
target:	shield
	the hilt of a sword made a cross-shape, and so was a proper sign on which to swear
points ... hose:	'points' are (1) swords and (2) the laces attaching hose to doublet—which gives point to Poins's pun
Kendal green:	coarse cloth worn by lower-class country people
knotty-pated:	block-headed
tallow-catch:	dripping-pan, or perhaps 'tallow keech', the lump of tallow rolled up by butchers to make candles
strappado:	a form of torture in which a man was hoisted up by his arms tied behind his back, and dropped abruptly, with the effect (at least) of dislocating his shoulders. The word is of French or Spanish origin
sanguine coward:	this is a paradox, since the sanguine temperament (which Falstaff clearly has) was supposed to be courageous

'sblood ... standing-tuck: Falstaff retorts to the Prince's abuse of his fatness by a string of comparisons for the Prince's tall, skinny build

neat's tongue: ox. tongue

pizzle: penis

stock-fish: dried cod

standing-tuck: upright rapier

starting hole: bolt-hole, hiding-place

Lion ... prince: a widespread belief

nobleman ... royal man: a well worn joke: a noble was a coin worth six shillings and eightpence, a royal ten shillings

taken with the manner: a legal term: 'in possession of the stolen property'

fire: an allusion to Bardolph's red face

meteors ... exhalations: Bardolph compares his own face to meteors and shooting-stars

hot ... purses: drinking heats the liver and empties the purse

choler ... halter: Bardolph asserts that his red face is a sign of a choleric temperament. He is indicating that the Prince's insults will make him angry. The Prince responds with the familiar pun on choler: collar: halter implying that Bardolph will be hanged

bombast: padding used (often excessively) in fashionable clothes. But the metaphorical sense of bragging is also present

Sir John Bracy: he does not appear to have any historical original

Amamon: a devil with powers in the east

bastinado: a beating; strictly, on the soles of the feet

cross of a Welsh hook: the Welsh reaping-hook does not have a 'cross' as the hilt of a sword does

Well, that rascal ... for running: a quibble on running and running away

blue-caps: Scots, who wore knitted woollen hats dyed blue: 'blue bonnets'

stinking mackerel: mackerel are cheap and excellent fish, but go bad quickly

Why, then ... hundreds: it is a commonplace that war brings famine and plundering: girls who have nothing else will sell themselves for food. Hot weather was (and is) thought to increase sexual appetite

state: throne

leaden dagger: a dagger made of lead would be for show, not use, as the metal is too soft to inflict any injury

King Cambyses' vein: in the manner of an absurd ranting play of some thirty or more years earlier

leg: bow

harlotry: vulgar, unchaste, but here probably appreciative, as, for example, 'bastard' is sometimes a term of endearment amongst Australians

tickle-brain: a kind of strong drink

Harry ... his name: Falstaff's speech here is a parody of the artificial style made fashionable by the English writer John Lyly (1554?–1606) with his prose narrative *Euphues* (1579)

micher: a truant from school

rabbit-sucker: baby rabbit

poulter's hare: hare for sale in a poulterer's shop

a tun of man: the reference is both to Falstaff's drinking (a tun of wine is nearly 1000 litres) and his weight (ton)

trunk of humours: body full of diseases

bolting-hutch: a large box or bin for sifting flour

bombard: a large leather wine-container

cloak-bag: bag for carrying clothes; kit bag

Manningtree: a town in Essex, famous for its fairs, morality plays, and fat cattle

pudding: stuffing

reverend ... years: vice, iniquity and vanity are typical type-names of characters in the morality plays

I do, I will: at the end of *2 Henry IV* the Prince does banish Falstaff

watch: band of citizens called on to assist in keeping the peace or capturing criminals

devil ... fiddle-stick: 'the devil is responsible for this upset'

Never ... so: a difficult passage. It is evidently an appeal by Falstaff to the Prince to protect him

I deny ... another: 'I am not a coward. If you won't save me, then I'll show my courage by the way I behave when I am hanged'

arras: cloth wall-hangings. They were held on frames clear of the walls (to keep them free of damp) and so provided convenient concealment

above: see Introduction, p.11

hue and cry: outcry calling for the pursuit of a felon

Paul's: St Paul's Cathedral, London

anchovies: small, strongly-flavoured fish, often eaten as an accompaniment to drinking

ob: obolus; a halfpenny

charge of foot: the command of a company of infantry

his death ... score: 'to walk even twelve score [paces] will be enough to kill Falstaff'

Act III Scene 1 [Bangor. The Archdeacon's house]

This scene shows us the conspirators at home. It is also the only appearance (allowing for Shakespeare's conflation of two Edmund Mortimers—the uncle and the nephew—into one person) of the legitimate claimant to Henry IV's crown. The scene develops the political theme of the play. It opens with a clash of temperaments between Hotspur and Glendower. Hotspur's provocation is sympathetic to the audience—for a Welsh Nationalist in Elizabethan England would certainly have been a traitor—but he is also clearly in the wrong, and is reprimanded for his behaviour by both Mortimer and Worcester. Glendower shows the greater tact by letting Hotspur have his way. The occasion of the meeting is a treaty between Mortimer, Glendower and Hotspur for the division of England as the price of support of Mortimer's claim against Henry IV. The tone of the scene is quite bland, but it needs to be understood in the implicit context of Tudor insistence on national unity and the many speeches in Shakespeare's history plays which stress this theme (an example is John of Gaunt's deathbed speech in *Richard II*). To plan to divide England is the most extreme political folly and wickedness, and Mortimer's willingness to consider it is clear evidence that, however valid his claim to the throne, he is not a fit person to be king. The point is underlined by the flippant irresponsibility of Hotspur's cavilling over boundaries. The only consequence of such division would be further civil war.

When Hotspur has made his point, and been gratified by Glendower's giving way, he forgets his quarrel. The scene ends on an elegiac and domestic note. The romantic love between Mortimer and his Welsh wife, who cannot understand each other's speech, is contrasted with the affectionate sparring of Kate and Hotspur. However, Hotspur's impatient exit at the end of the scene suggests a return of his earlier mood. Mortimer's total disappearance from the play after this scene is not even commented upon. His intention was to accompany Hotspur to Shrewsbury (ll. 79–80). The chronicles offer no information either.

NOTES AND GLOSSARY:
No location is given in the quartos and folios: the information (which has no real bearing on the action) is derived from Holinshed by editors.

induction: beginning

cousin Glendower ... Hotspur: the leaders of the conspiracy are polite to each other: the actual relationship, by way of Hotspur's marriage to Mortimer's sister/aunt and Mortimer's marriage to Glendower's daughter, is very tenuous. The politeness does not last long

The front ... coward: the portents related to Glendower's birth are apparently Shakespeare's invention, as is the soldier-scholar-poet-magician who is developed in this scene. The Glendower of the chronicles is a barbarian

read to me: instructed me

Can trace ... experiments: 'can follow my tracks in time-consuming study of secret learning, or perform such powerful spells as I can'. The sixteenth-century senses of 'art' and 'experiments' are very difficult to convey: magic was believed in then much as we believe in science today

speaks better Welsh: a complicated insult: to the English Welsh was incomprehensible nonsense; at the same time Welshmen were supposed to be incorrigible boasters. The only talent Hotspur allows Glendower is that he can speak his own ridiculous language

bootless: unsuccessful. Hotspur makes the obvious pun in the following line. The bad Welsh weather, according to Holinshed, was caused '(as was thought) through art magick'

Come ... from Trent: the division of the kingdom, as is clear from earlier and later plays like *Gorboduc* and *King Lear*, is a terrible crime and will lead to disaster

indentures ... interchangeable: a copy of the agreement was made for each of the three parties, and each was signed (and sealed) by all three (see note on l.135 below)

moiety: share

cantle: segment

smug: smooth. The modern sense of 'self-satisfied' was not developed at this time

bottom: good-quality flat land by a river

It shall not ... that will I: the dispute is ridiculous and suggests a confusion of the territory with the map. Worcester's 'little charge' would in fact involve civil engineering work on a scale unknown in England from the time of the Romans to the eighteenth-century canal-builders

Gelding ... much: cutting as much from the other side

canstick: candlestick

dry: needing grease

mincing: dancing affectedly

forced ... nag: the uneasy motion of a horse that does not pick its feet up properly

Come . . . land: once Hotspur has won his point, and made Glendower give way, he is satisfied. He covets dominance, not land. It is possible to sympathise with his irritation at Glendower's self-praise, but Glendower's absence from Shrewsbury may be partly a response to Hotspur's provocation

indentures drawn: the copies for all the parties were written on the same sheet, and then torn apart (drawn). Matching the 'indentures' of the torn edges of the paper demonstrated the genuineness of the documents

moldwarp: mole

Merlin: the great magician of Welsh legend

And of a dragon ... cat: prophesies are commonly phrased in vague symbolic language, which needs skilled interpretation. The dragon was Glendower's heraldic animal, the lion Percy's

skimble-skamble: this word seems to be Shakespeare's invention: nonsensical

several: various

smoky house: proverbially associated with a 'railing wife' as intolerable

cheese and garlic: the diet of the very poor

windmill: a noisy and unstable dwelling

cates: delicacies

summer house: a house for pleasure and entertainment

well ... concealments: learned and skilful in occult matters

mines of India: the gold and silver mines of the Spanish Indies in America

too wilful-blame: too much to blame for wilfulness

blood: high courage; spirit

opinion: obstinacy in opinion

aunt Percy: Glendower's son-in-law and confederate in rebellion was Lady Percy's brother, not nephew. Lady Percy was aunt to Richard II's nominated heir, but he was not married to Glendower's daughter. It is another instance of the confusion of two Edmund Mortimers (see I.3.79, 83–4, 144)

harlotry: a term of abuse here used affectionately and without any sexual implication (compare II.4.390)

I understand ... thee: 'I understand the language of tears that flows from your eyes, and I could weep too, if I were not ashamed of being unmanly'

division: a passage of rapid playing, a variation on a slower theme

wanton:	lush, comfortable; but also probably a transferred epithet 'lie down in a wanton manner on the rushes'
humorous:	capricious
Then ... humours:	if the 'humorous' devil is a good musician, then, says Lady Percy, Hotspur should be an even better musician, for he is even more impulsive and capricious, more governed by his 'humours' than the devil is
brach:	hound bitch
be still:	'be silent', but also 'stop playing the fool' and 'don't fidget'. The whole exchange has sexual implications as well
Not yours ... citizens:	Hotspur condemns his wife's mild asseverations as middle-class: as a lady of real breeding she should swear properly
comfit-maker:	confectioner
sarcenet:	thin silk cloth, therefore insubstantial
Finsbury:	Finsbury Fields, north of London, where tradesmen and their wives went for Sunday walks in their best clothes
pepper-gingerbread:	cheap gingerbread, not the real thing, as Kate's oaths are not
'Tis the next ... ye will:	Hotspur's 'humour' changes again; he drops his quibbling with Kate, and impatiently leaves
tailor:	tailors sang at their work
redbreast:	robin. These birds have a powerful and attractive song

---

Act III Scene 2 [London. The palace]

The reality of the scene between the Prince and his father is not much like the rehearsal shown in II.4. King Henry IV first suggests that the Prince's bad behaviour is because he is marked:

> For the hot vengeance and the rod of heaven,
> To punish my mistreadings.

The Prince acknowledges faults, but at the same time suggests that the reports reaching the King may be malicious and exaggerated. The King launches into a long lecture on his own discreet behaviour as a young man, compared with the self-display and folly of Richard II. He goes on to say that as he was in comparison to Richard then, so Hotspur is in comparison to Prince Henry now. A eulogy of Hotspur's successes in battle follows, ending with the suggestion that Prince Hal might be willing to support the rebels against his father. This at last provokes the

Prince to a vehement reply, and the assertion that in the coming battle he will justify himself and defeat Hotspur. The scene ends with reconciliation and the brisk arrangement of the movement of the royal forces to Shrewsbury to meet the rebels.

NOTES AND GLOSSARY:

I know not ... heart: the King suggests that Prince Henry's bad behaviour is a judgement of God upon himself: such low tastes and behaviour in one so well born and educated are otherwise inexplicable. The King's own guilty conscience is implicit here, and so is the text (basic to the whole Tudor view of history) 'The sins of the fathers shall be visited upon the children'.The punishment for the King's sins will fall upon the Prince, and, at the same time, the Prince, by his dissolute behaviour, *is* the punishment for the King's sins

inordinate: disorderly

attempts: exploits

So please ... submission: the Prince acknowledges some faults, but suggests that the King has heard much about him which is not true. He asks that the real offences may be treated more leniently, if he can demonstrate that much he is charged with is false

reproof: disproof

pickthanks ... newsmongers: sycophants, spreaders of rumour

affections: tendencies

rudely lost: traditionally, the act which lost the Prince his place on the Council was the act of striking the Lord Chief Justice. Shakespeare's omission of this is part of his rehabilitation of the Prince

common-hackneyed: made common like an overworked horse

possession: both the possessor and his right; that is, Richard II

bavin: a bundle of twigs which would burn brightly, but soon go out

carded his state: degraded his status

against his name: to the detriment of his reputation and title

stand the push: submit to the impudence

comparative: person who makes (insulting) comparisons

Enfeoff'd: gave himself up

cuckoo ... June: the cuckoo is a migratory bird, and its first arrival in England in spring time with its very distinctive call is still earnestly noted, with letters to the newspapers. By June, its call is commonplace, and unnoticed

community: commonness, familiarity

sun-like: the King in the State was thought to correspond to the sun in the heavens

aspect: appearance

cloudy: sullen, dismal. The same metaphors run through the King's speech here as are found in the Prince's soliloquy at the end of I.2

vile participation: mixing with low people

He hath ... succession: Hotspur's worth—his reputation as a soldier—gives him a better claim to the throne than Prince Henry's right of succession. This is a 'shadow' because of his bad reputation, but also perhaps the King's metaphor recognises unconsciously that the claim of succession is indeed shadowy, since Henry IV was not the lawful successor to Richard II

colour: appearance

harness: armour—and therefore armed soldiers

Turns ... jaws: raises an army against the royal power. The lion is the king of beasts, as well as the heraldic beast still found on the English royal standard

being ... thou: the historical Hotspur was in fact older than Henry IV himself

Against ... Christ: Douglas is acknowledged the best soldier in Christendom

Thrice: this seems generous, since one of the major engagements, Otterburn, was a defeat for the English, and Hotspur was captured

Mars in swathling clothes: 'infant warrior'. Mars is the Roman god of war. Infants were customarily 'swathed' (or swaddled)—wrapped firmly in a long strip of cloth that restricted movement. The infant Jesus is sometimes so represented in Renaissance painting because of the references in Luke 2:7 and 12, in the Bible

Enlarged ... throne: Douglas was captured at Holmedon, though this is scarcely explicit at I.1.70–4. The advice to release prisoners without ransom is given by Worcester at I.3.255–6

Capitulate: make a treaty. The original meaning was to make any formal agreement, where the matters agreed were drawn up under different headings (Latin *caput*: head). The use became restricted to treaties of submission, and the common modern meaning is simply 'surrender'

nearest and dearest: this common phrase for members of the immediate family circle is given paradoxical force by 'enemy'. 'Dearest' may also have the sense 'most costly'

vassal fear: fear appropriate to a low-born person, not a prince

base inclination: both 'inclination to be base' and 'the sort of inclination a menial person would have'

start of spleen: fit of ill-temper (compare II.3.79)

favours: features; perhaps also the insignia by which a man in armour identified himself

honour ... helm: the reputation Hotspur has won is seen as a crest decorating his helmet (compare V.4.71)

factor: agent

parcel: part

Mortimer of Scotland: Shakespeare means the Scottish Earl of March, who was a Dunbar, and not related in any way to the family of Mortimer, the English Earl of March. 'March' in both titles means the frontier and country near it. The Mortimers were the hereditary guardians of the English frontier with Wales; the Dunbars of the Scottish frontier with England

advertisement: news

On Wednesday ... meet: the Prince is sent out a day ahead, and given a slightly longer route to Shrewsbury than the main road to be taken by the King. This is presumably to give the two armies better facilities for provisioning themselves and impressing soldiers as they go (compare IV.2.)

Our business valued: all things considered

Act III Scene 3 [Eastcheap. The Boar's Head Tavern]

Falstaff is in low spirits and jokes rather peevishly with Bardolph. When the Hostess enters he takes up with her the loss of his ring and the papers taken from him while he was asleep at the end of II.4. The value has been grossly inflated. The Hostess in reply complains of his long-standing debts to her. When the Prince enters he resolves the quarrel by acknowledging that he picked Falstaff's pocket. The scene ends with energetic preparations for the march to Shrewsbury. As in the other tavern scenes, the jokes are difficult to elucidate, since they often depend on obscure and archaic puns.

NOTES AND GLOSSARY:

Bardolph ... apple-john: Falstaff complains—probably quite falsely—that he has lost weight

apple-john: a long-keeping apple, the skin of which became wrinkled during storage

suddenly: straight away

in some liking: (1) in the mood; (2) in fair condition

out of heart: (1) lacking courage, or inclination; (2) in bad condition

brewer's horse: brewers were proverbial for using worn-out, ancient horses, only skin and bone

so fretful: worry so much

virtuously given: inclined towards virtue

in good compass: within reasonable limits. Bardolph (l.21) applies it to Falstaff's physical circumference

admiral: flagship

poop: highest part of the stern of a ship. The 'lantern in the poop' was to give direction to other ships

in the nose: Bardolph has the red grog blossom nose of the alcoholic

Knight of the Burning Lamp: a parody of the kind of title found in the then popular romances of chivalry

death's-head: skull, or representation of one

memento mori: reminder of death

Dives: the rich man who ended up in hell in the parable of Dives and Lazarus (see the Bible, Luke 16:19–31)

I never ... angel: Falstaff plays with the alternative heavenly and hellish implications of fire and light

ignis fatuus: the light produced by the spontaneous combustion of gas produced by decaying vegetable matter sometimes seen over swamps

ball of wildfire: fiercely burning projectile used in warfare; also a kind of firework and a skin disease producing circular red eruptions

perpetual ... bonfire-light: a never ending display of fireworks: but 'bonfire' in Shakespeare's day still retained its original sense of funeral pyre, or fire on which heretics were burned

links: brightly burning flares, carried to light travellers through the streets at night

drunk me: drunk at my expense

as good cheap: as cheaply

chandler: dealer in candles, and by extension any tradesman

salamander: mythical lizard-like reptile supposed to be able to live in fire

in your belly: a proverbial retort about anything complained of (compare the vulgar modern 'stuff it')

be heart-burnt:	get indigestion
Partlet the hen:	a woman upset about something is traditionally compared to a clucking hen
Partlet:	is traditional; the name of the hen in Chaucer's *Nun's Priest's Tale*
tithe:	tenth part
a woman:	Falstaff is perhaps suggesting no more than the general untrustworthiness of women, but Mistress Quickly understands him to mean a prostitute
know:	this too can carry a sexual meaning
Dowlas:	cheap, coarse linen
bolters:	sieves to separate bran from meal
holland:	best quality fine linen
ell:	the 'ell' in England was a measure of forty-five inches. Cloth of this price would have been of the very highest quality
diet:	meals. Falstaff was a regular boarder at the Boar's Head
by-drinkings:	drinks in addition to those normally supplied with meals
rich:	a red face at this time was called a 'rich' face
denier:	one-tenth of a penny; the least valuable coin
younker:	inexperienced youth to be taken advantage of
seal-ring:	often a valued heirloom
mark:	a coin worth two-thirds of a pound
Jack:	a low-class fellow
sneak-up:	a coward
truncheon:	[stage direction] a short, stout stick
Is ... door:	does the wind blow that way; is that what is going to happen?
Newgate fashion:	prisoners going to or from Newgate prison were chained in pairs
bawdy-house:	brothel
stewed prune:	brothel-keeper. There is plenty of evidence for this odd association: perhaps prunes were regarded as a prophylactic diet against venereal disease
drawn fox:	most probably a hunted fox, which had been drawn from cover, and which would display great cunning in attempting to escape
Maid Marian:	the female character, played by a man in May game and Morris dance, represented often enough, no doubt, with gross indecency
deputy's ... ward:	wife of the most responsible citizen of a particular district

thing:	almost certainly had the implication of prostitute, as indicated by Mistress Quickly's indignant rejection of the statement that she is 'a thing to thank God on'
on:	for
otter:	something equivocal, as the context makes clear. Mistress Otter in Jonson's *Silent Woman* is a virago who bullies her subservient husband
where to have her:	how to understand her. However, the Hostess's reply, where she intends 'where to have me' to mean 'how to take advantage of me', can again carry sexual innuendo, as the Prince's rapid response implies
ought:	archaic form for 'owed'
but as ... whelp:	compare II.4.267–71
I ... break:	a quite frequent oath
Midriff:	diaphragm
embossed rascal:	the basic meaning is 'swollen rogue', but in hunting terms a 'rascal' is a young deer of inferior quality, and 'embossed' means foaming at the mouth
injuries:	things the loss of which is the injury Falstaff complains of
you ... pocket?:	Falstaff, as usual, makes some advantage out of his defeat
still:	as usual, as I always am
with unwashed hands:	proverbial: without delay
I would ... virtuous:	Falstaff at once sees the war as a means for his own advantage
Go ... afternoon:	notice the change in the Prince to brisk efficiency
furniture:	equipment
drum:	troops assembled 'to the drum'. Falstaff would like to go to war without leaving the tavern

---

Act IV Scene 1 [Shrewsbury. The rebel camp]

Hotspur and Douglas are paying each other compliments when a letter is brought from Northumberland announcing that he is sick and unable to bring his army to Shrewsbury. Worcester is disturbed, but Douglas and particularly Hotspur quickly regain confidence. Sir Richard Vernon arrives with news of the approach of the royal armies. In reply to a scornful enquiry from Hotspur he launches into a eulogy of a reformed Prince Henry as an ideal warrior. Hotspur responds with a passage of 'valiant rant'. Finally comes more bad news: Glendower, too, is unable to keep his promises, and his army will not be ready for another fourteen days.

NOTES AND GLOSSARY:

attribution:	praise
As not ... world:	the image is of coining. The present events ('the season's stamp') turn men into soldiers. Douglas is a soldier of such quality that he is like a coin that would be accepted anywhere in the world
soothers:	flatterers
No man ... him:	Douglas's reply—'if there is any man alive as good as you, I will confront him'—sounds fine, but makes rather odd sense
He did ... physicians:	'When I left he had been confined to bed for four days, and his doctors were very worried about him'
better worth:	of more value
sickness:	there seems to be a break in the sense here. This may be an omission in the text, or it may be an indication that Hotspur is skimming the contents of his letter
by deputation:	by a deputy (because Northumberland was too ill to act himself)
list:	edge; literally the selvedge of cloth
hair:	kind, species
brooks:	tolerates
loyalty:	to the King
mere:	simple
apprehension:	idea; and perhaps also fear
strict arbitrement:	careful investigation and judgement
loop:	hole
draws a curtain:	and so reveals
make a head:	raise a revolution
daft ... aside:	brushed aside
All furnished ... horsemanship:	Vernon's eulogy of Prince Henry combines praise for practical strength and skill with high imagery appropriate to royalty. To leap in full armour into the saddle required skill as well as great strength. 'Turning' and 'winding' are technical terms used in the management of horses: the images of eagles, gold, and midsummer sun are all appropriate to royalty, while the references to 'May', 'youthful goats' and 'young bulls' suggest youth and strength and agility
furnished:	equipped for war
estridges:	ostriches
Bated:	beat their wings
eagles ... bathed:	eagles were supposed to renew their plumage by bathing in the ocean

glittering ... images:	statues or memorial effigies were often gilded and brightly painted
beaver:	faceguard on a helmet
cushes:	cuisses, thigh armour
Mercury:	messenger of the gods, equipped with wings on his hat and heels
Pegasus:	the winged horse of Greek mythology
worse ... agues:	the spring is generally the time of epidemics: cold weather, on the whole, restricts the spread of germs. Hotspur says that this praise of Prince Henry makes him tremble as if he had a spring fever
like ... trim:	like animals decorated for sacrifice, and will be slaughtered in the same way
fire-ey'd ... war:	Bellona, the Roman goddess of war
Mars:	the Roman god of war
reprisal:	plunder
taste:	try out, test
corse:	corpse
draw his power:	gather his forces. According to Holinshed Glendower was at the battle of Shrewsbury
battle:	army

Act IV Scene 2 [A road near Coventry]

The location of the scene and what is happening are indicated in the opening speech: Falstaff is on his way to Shrewsbury with his 'charge of foot'. Bardolph is sent off to buy wine, while Falstaff in soliloquy explains how he turns the power he has to impress the soldiers for the King's army to his own advantage. Prince Henry and Westmoreland enter, and there is comment on the need for haste: 'Percy is already in the field'.

NOTES AND GLOSSARY:

Coventry:	a town in the midlands of England, not far from Shakespeare's home town of Stratford-upon-Avon
Sutton Co'fil':	Sutton Coldfield is twenty miles from Coventry— but it is not on the road from Coventry to Shrewsbury
lay out:	'pay from your own pocket'
makes an angel:	brings the amount I have spent up to an angel—a coin worth one third of a pound
answer the coinage:	be responsible for the cost
soused:	cooked or pickled in vinegar
gurnet:	gurnard, a small fish; also a term of abuse

If I ... hedge: Falstaff's account of his use of the power of impressment refers to current Elizabethan abuses. England was engaged in endemic conflicts in Holland, France and Ireland throughout this period, although never involved in a major war after the failure of the Spanish Armada. Quite simply, Falstaff presses the most well-to-do and unwilling he can find, and then accepts bribes to let them off. In their places he takes down-and-outs, dead-beats, petty criminals and gaol-birds

contracted: engaged to be married

banns: the announcement in church of an intended marriage, made on three consecutive Sundays before the ceremony, so that any objections can be heard

lief: willingly

caliver: light gun

toasts-and-butter: well fed and consequently lazy and cowardly people

ancients: ensigns, standard-bearers

gentlemen of companies: men who, because of birth or connections, could not be called common soldiers in a very hierarchical society, but at the same time did not rank as officers

Lazarus in the painted cloth: see III.3.30. 'Painted cloth' was a cheap substitute for tapestry for wall-hangings, and representations of this parable were popular

never soldiers: only the officers, non-commissioned officers and 'gentlemen' in Falstaff's 'charge' have any experience of warfare

discarded ... trade-fallen: domestic servants dismissed for dishonesty, young men with no inheritance, run-away barmen and out-of-work stable hands

cankers of a calm world and a long peace: long peace allowed bad 'humours' to accumulate in the body politic, as sloth did in the physical body. The cankers produced by this political disease—the unemployed and disaffected citizens—could be used, and got rid of, in a war

old fazed ancient: old tattered flag

prodigals ... husks: an allusion to the parable in the Bible of the Prodigal Son, Luke 15:11–32

draff: refuse

gibbets: gallows. The bodies of executed criminals were hung in chains at conspicuous places as a warning. Local place-names like 'Gallows Corner', 'Gibbet Heath' or 'Hanging Hill' still exist in England

gyves:	leg-chains
Saint Albans ... Daventry:	both towns on the road between London and Coventry, a road with which Shakespeare himself was familiar
linen enough on every hedge:	washing spread to dry on hedgerows was easy to steal
blown:	(1) inflated, (2) short-winded, out of breath
quilt:	a pun on Jack, which was the name for a soldier's quilted leather coat
I think ... butter:	'since you are as fat as butter no doubt you have stolen plenty of cream already'
food for powder:	cannon-fodder. Falstaff's soldiers are expendable (see below, V.3.37)
bare ... bareness:	Westmoreland refers to their lack of decent clothes; Falstaff interprets 'bare' in the sense of thin, emaciated
three fingers in the ribs:	fat three fingers deep over your ribs. A finger as linear measure was about three-quarters of an inch. Four fingers made a hand. It is still conventional to give the height of a horse in England in hands, though the hand is now standardised at four inches
fray:	fight

Act IV Scene 3 [Shrewsbury. The rebel camp]

The leaders of the rebels are debating tactics. Hotspur and Douglas want immediate action, while Worcester and Vernon recommend delay, until more of their forces are available, and are better rested. Sir Walter Blunt comes as an embassy from King Henry with the offer of pardon and the rapid redress of any just grievance. Hotspur is sceptical about this offer, and recounts the Percy view of how Henry came from exile with the help and support of Northumberland and how when he had usurped the throne and killed the King he turned against those who had helped him. After this outburst Hotspur becomes placatory, and proposes that Worcester shall go in the morning to the King's camp for further parley. It appears from this scene that Hotspur is the spokesman for the rebels, and also that he is inconsistent since the proposal for Worcester's embassy in the morning is incompatible with Hotspur's earlier support for an attack 'tonight'.

NOTES AND GLOSSARY:

supply:	reinforcements
If ... on:	'If real honour, and not mere vanity or rashness, is in question'

men ... leading: such reputable and experienced leaders
drag ... expedition: prevent us acting swiftly
journey-bated: worn out with travelling
quality: party
defend: forbid
out of limit and true rule: in breach of loyalty or proper order
suggestion: instigation. The word at this time almost always means bad suggestion
sue his livery: petition for the release of his lands, which, on the death of his father, John of Gaunt, reverted to the Crown; a legal technicality
with cap and knee: with cap in hand and on one knee, in deference
as greatness knows itself: as he became conscious of his own greatness
me: this is an example of the 'ethical dative'. Its function here is emphatic, if anything; also at line 85
straight: strict
face: appearance
in deputation: as his deputies
personal: personally present as commander
task'd: taxed, though there is a slight technical difference between taxing and 'tasking'
March: Edmund Mortimer, Richard II's heir-designate, conflated with his uncle in this play
engaged: held as hostage
intelligence: here in the secret service sense, spies
Rated ... council-board: compare I.3.14–20
In rage ... court: compare I.3.120–22
head of safety: uprising for our own safety
indirect: not in the direct line of succession
and ... shall: after his outburst Hotspur is surprisingly mild

---

Act IV Scene 4 [York. The Archbishop's Palace]

This brief scene, in which we see the Archbishop of York making preparations to meet the possibility of a royal victory at Shrewsbury, is a significant link with *2 Henry IV*, where these rebels in their turn are defeated. At the same time (for the spectator who does not know the story) it increases suspense about the outcome and gives further emphasis to the efficiency of King Henry compared to the poor organisation of the rebels.

NOTES AND GLOSSARY:
Sir Michael: unknown; perhaps a knight, but 'Sir' was often used as a courtesy title for priests

brief:	letter
lord marshal:	Thomas Mowbray, Duke of Norfolk, one of the rebel leaders in *2 Henry IV*
cousin Scroop:	this might be any of several relatives of the Archbishop, Richard Scroop; compare I.3.265
bide the touch:	be tested, as gold was tested with a touchstone
Lord Harry:	Hotspur
first proportion:	biggest section: Northumberland's troops would have made the bulk of the rebel army
rated sinew:	valued strength
prophecies:	apparently Shakespeare's invention, appropriate to the character he gives Glendower
Mortimer:	he intended (III.1.78–80) to travel to Shrewsbury with Hotspur. No explanation of his absence is provided
moe:	more
corrivals:	associates
dear men:	men of distinction

Act V Scene 1 [Shrewsbury. The King's camp]

This scene involves the morning parley proposed at the end of IV.3. Worcester and Vernon come to the King's camp and Worcester is spokesman for the rebel cause. The King receives it coldly, but Prince Henry proposes single combat between himself and Hotspur as a resolution of the dispute, instead of a general battle. The King confirms this and adds vague general offers for the redress of grievances. The embassy departs, and the scene ends with a brief exchange between the Prince and Falstaff, and then Falstaff's famous soliloquy on 'honour'.

NOTES AND GLOSSARY:

bulky:	large, looming. Many editions read 'busky' (wooded)—following Q2 and later editions
distemperature:	sickness (compare the image of the obscured sun— of royalty in eclipse—I.2.192–3)
southern:	the south wind was supposed to be unhealthy
old limbs:	the historical Henry was not old
obedient orb:	an analogy between the social and the astronomical order: the planets in their ordered movements relative to the sun were like great lords around the King. The 'meteor' (l.19) is the 'portent' (l.20) as well as the example of disorder. The analogy survives as a dead metaphor in phrases like 'the proper sphere of influence'

exhaled: dragged from the orderly course proper to heavenly bodies. Meteors were thought to be caused by the sun drawing up vapours from the earth, and so were 'exhaled' in this sense, also, and the image related back to the mists that make the rising sun look red and distempered in the opening speech

broached: opened, set going

dislike: discord

chewet: (1) jackdaw, someone who talks at the wrong time, (2) meat pie, another reference to Falstaff's bulk

remember: remind

staff of office: Worcester was Steward to the Royal Household of Richard II; breaking the white staff of office signified his defection from Richard

no: a double negative with 'nor'. Modern usage would be 'any'

new-fall'n right: his inheritance from his father, John of Gaunt, who had recently died

gull, the cuckoo's bird: nestling, offspring of the cuckoo

sparrow: the hedge-sparrow, not the much commoner house-sparrow, is often chosen as a host by the parasitic cuckoo

fear of swallowing: of being swallowed. The cuckoo was reputed (incorrectly) to devour the birds that fostered it

dangerous countenance: threatening looks

face: trim, decorate

colour: pretence; but facings of a 'fine colour' would make a 'garment' (l.74) attractive

discontents: discontented people

rub the elbow: apparently considered as a sign of pleasure

hurlyburly innovation: change which throws everything into confusion. 'Innovation' almost invariably had a bad sense at this time

Water-colours: these are bad because they are quickly applied but do not last; since 'colour' still has the sense of pretence, 'water-colours' are thin and weak pretences

moody: sullen, angry

in trial: in contest, battle

by my hopes: 'as I hope for salvation'

set off his head: not held against him

yet this before my father's majesty: the Prince calls the King to witness the solemnity and sincerity of his challenge

albeit: although

cousin's:	used freely for blood relations: here equivalent to 'nephew's'
and will they:	and if they will
Rebuke ... us:	defeat and terrible punishment are our servants
take it advisedly:	consider it carefully
colossus:	giant; from the large statue of Apollo at Rhodes, which is reputed to have stood across the entrance to the harbour
thou ... death:	proverbial: everyone must die
pay ... day:	pay the debt before it is due
pricks ... prick:	in the first case to urge on, as a horse, with spurs; in the second, to mark down for destruction
set to:	replace if cut off, or set, as a broken bone
grief:	pain
insensible:	not to be perceived by the senses
detraction:	slander, malicious gossip
scutcheon:	decoration for a funeral in the shape of a shield painted with a coat of arms

Act V Scene 2 [Shrewsbury. The rebel camp]

On the return to the rebel camp Worcester persuades Vernon that the King's offer of amnesty and the redress of grievances must not be reported to Hotspur: the King is not to be trusted to keep his word. Vernon supports Worcester's claim, 'There is no seeming mercy in the King', and Westmoreland, who had been engaged as a hostage for the safe return of Worcester and Vernon, is sent back with a message of defiance. The Prince of Wales's challenge to Hotspur is reported, and Vernon praises his modest and chivalrous behaviour. The scene ends with an exhortation from Hotspur as the battle begins.

NOTES AND GLOSSARY:

supposition:	suspicion
full of eyes:	Argus, the herdsman who guarded Io for the jealous Hera in Greek mythology, had eyes all over his body. After his death they were put in the peacock's tail
Interpretation ... looks:	a damaging interpretation will be put on our looks
adopted name of privilege:	his nickname allows him to be rash
spleen:	see note on II.3.79
Westmoreland:	this is the first indication that Westmoreland is the 'surety for a safe return' (IV.3.109) of Worcester and Vernon

seeming:	appearance
engaged:	held as a surety
tasking:	challenge
duties of a man:	what is due to a man
dispraising ... you:	praise could not do justice to your merits
cital:	recital, account
instantly:	both at the same time
envy:	the dangers of the coming battle
so wild a liberty:	such wild libertinism
Better ... persuasion:	Hotspur's syntax is very condensed: 'consider for yourselves what you have to do and you will raise your own spirits higher than I can raise them, since I am no orator'
I ... now:	Hotspur's impatience is typical, and again irresponsible
If ... hour:	if life were only one hour long. Most clocks at this period had only an hour-hand
Esperance:	the Percy war-cry (compare II.3.72)
heaven to earth:	the odds [that some of them will die that day] are as great as heaven to earth

---

Act V Scene 3 [Shrewsbury. The field of battle]

This scene break is editorial, first made by Capell in 1767. The action of the battle is to be thought of as continuous and the stage not specifically localised. The original folio stage direction reads: 'They embrace, the trumpets sound, the King enters with his power, alarum to the battle. Then enter Douglas and Sir Walter Blunt.'

Blunt, disguised as the King, is killed by Douglas, who has already killed one false King. Hotspur recognises Blunt as another impersonation, and he and Douglas depart. Falstaff appears, having left his men in a dangerous situation; an impatient Prince Henry urges him back to the battle, borrows his pistol and finds a bottle, instead of a gun, in the case.

NOTES AND GLOSSARY:

Stafford:	Holinshed names Stafford as killed by Douglas, and also says that Douglas killed Blunt and three others appearing to be the King, but he does not say that Stafford was one of them
a fool go with:	a proverbial phrase, meaning 'may you be called a fool wherever you go'
whither:	wherever
shot-free	without paying the bill

scoring:	getting goods on credit (compare II.4.27). Falstaff typically makes puns on the danger of his being 'shot' or having his head gashed open. The 'score' was originally kept—and sometimes still is—with notches cut in a tally-stick
there's ... vanity!:	the dead Sir Walter Blunt is an example of what honour is really like
bowels:	guts
there's ... alive:	it was to Falstaff's advantage to get his men killed off: he would keep their pay. The abuse of keeping dead men on the muster rolls for this purpose was often condemned
to beg:	they will be so badly injured that they will have no means of life but begging
Turk Gregory:	Turks are proverbial in this period for barbarity. No Turk Gregory is known and the reference is usually though to be—anachronistically—to Pope Gregory XIII (1572–85), who was a bitter enemy of England and offered absolution to any person who would murder Queen Elizabeth I
hot:	early pistols overheated with frequent use, and had to be allowed to cool down, but Falstaff means that the liquor in his bottle is 'hot stuff'
pierce:	pronounced 'perce'
carbonado:	barbecue

Act V Scene 4 [the same]

Although this scene division is marked in the folio (it is not in the quartos) the only unity of the scene comes from the fact that it begins and ends with a briefly empty stage. It is a linked series of episodes in the continuing battle. Initially the rebel forces have the advantage: the King has withdrawn from the battle, Prince Henry has been wounded—not seriously, it appears, for though he is bleeding he refuses to retire, but returns to the battle shortly after Prince John and Westmoreland. The King is left briefly alone, then attacked by Douglas. He is in danger when Prince Henry returns and fights Douglas who quickly runs away. There is a brief reconciliation: the King acknowledges that the Prince of Wales has saved his life. He leaves the scene and Hotspur enters. He and Prince Henry exchange vaunts and fight. Falstaff enters and cheers from the sidelines until he is attacked by Douglas. Falstaff 'falls down as if he were dead'. Prince Henry mortally wounds Hotspur, who has a dying speech, and then an epitaph from the Prince. On seeing Falstaff apparently dead, the Prince speaks another farewell, and leaves the stage. Falstaff revives, inflicts another wound on the dead Hotspur and is preparing to carry him off when Prince Henry returns with John of Lancaster. Falstaff brazenly maintains that he killed Hotspur, and is told that the Prince will 'gild' his lie.

NOTES AND GLOSSARY:

make up:	return to battle
amaze:	dismay
stained:	both literally, with blood and dirt, and dishonoured
ungrown warrior:	the historical John of Lancaster was about thirteen at the time of the battle of Shrewsbury. There is no evidence that he actually fought there
Hydra's heads:	in Greek mythology the second of the labours of Hercules was to kill the Hydra, a monster that lived in the Lernian swamp. This was difficult because as soon as one head was cut off the Hydra, two more grew in its place
Two ... sphere:	each of the planets had its own sphere in ptolemaic astronomy
well said:	well done
prophesy:	it was a common belief that dying men had the power of prophesy: so, in *Richard II*, John of Gaunt prophesies Richard's downfall
Ill-weav'd ... shrunk:	badly made cloth shrinks
favours:	some identifying ornament; perhaps a scarf or the three plumes, the 'Prince of Wales's feathers', on his crest
heavy:	the expected allusion to Falstaff's weight
dearer:	both worthier and better loved
embowelled:	disembowelled; prepared for embalming. There is also a continuing pun based on 'deer' (l.106), which were 'assayed' when disembowelled, to see how deep the fat on them was
in blood:	continues the puns on hunting: a deer 'in blood' was one in vigorous health—as, in fact, is the apparently dead Falstaff
powder:	pickle
scot and lot:	paid in full
better ... discretion:	a well known phrase, though its proberbial currency probably comes from Falstaff, and keeps his misinterpretation. The real sense is something like Vernon's 'well respected honour' (IV.3.10) midway between Falstaff's cowardice and Hotspur's foolhardiness

nothing ... eyes:	if I'm not observed, I cannot be found out
double-man:	a *Doppelgänger*, an apparition—but with allusion to Percy on his back
take ... death:	generally a serious oath
highest:	the highest ground
follow ... reward:	another hunting term: dogs were rewarded with certain parts when the deer was cut up
purge:	probably both physical and moral: go on a diet, get rid of excess humours and repent of my bad ways

Act V Scene 5 [the same]

The conclusion: the victorious King sentences Worcester and Vernon to death; Prince Henry chivalrously—but also with political wisdom—begs a free pardon for Douglas. The scene ends with decisions to follow up the victory by proceeding against Glendower and Mortimer in Wales and Northumberland and the Archbishop of York in the north. These are some of the concerns of *2 Henry IV*.

NOTES AND GLOSSARY:

rebuke:	shameful defeat
Three knights:	Holinshed mentions ten knights killed
upon ... fear:	running away in panic
divide our power:	split our forces
dearest speed:	as fast as you can
sway:	power

Part 3

Commentary

The history plays

Henry IV Part 1 is one of eight plays dealing in sequence with a century of English history, the period of the 'Wars of the Roses' from the reign of Richard II (1377–99; deposed by Henry IV and murdered in 1400) to the defeat and death of Richard III at the battle of Bosworth Field in 1485, and the establishment of the Tudor dynasty in the person of Henry VII, the grandfather of Elizabeth I. This is not the place to give more than the very briefest account of this total work, but to understand *1 Henry IV* properly we need to see that it has a place in a larger whole, a drama in eight plays that can be called 'epic' for its scope, its concern with national destiny, and for its shaping effect on later generations' understanding of England's past. The history of the fifteenth century is still seen by the English through Shakespeare's interpretation, even by those who have never read his plays. In spite of the rehabilitation attempted by serious historians, Richard III remains, for most people, the hunchbacked bogey who murdered the little princes in the Tower. Shakespeare's eight plays fall conveniently into two sets of four, often referred to as the first and second tetralogies. The earliest written plays are the three parts of *King Henry VI* and *Richard III*. Henry VI was the grandson of Henry IV (and so the son of Prince Henry in *Henry IV*). He was born in 1421 after the prince became king as Henry V, and only one year before his father's death. Rival factions during his infancy led to the loss of Henry V's conquests in France. Subsequent civil wars in England resulted in his deposition in favour of the Yorkist claimant of the throne, Edward IV, who reigned from 1461 to 1483, though there was a brief reinstatement of Henry VI in the year before his murder in 1471.

The 'Wars of the Roses' take their title from the emblems—the white rose and the red— of the leaders of the rival factions, the Dukes of York and Lancaster. The dynastic basis of the prolonged power struggle is set out by Shakespeare in *2 Henry VI*, Act II, Scene 2, lines 1–52:

YORK: Now my good Lords of Salisbury and Warwick,
            Our simple supper ended, give me leave,
            In this close walk to satisfy myself
            In craving your opinion of my title,
            Which is infallible, to England's crown.
SAL.:   My Lord, I long to hear it at full.

WAR.: Sweet York, begin; and if thy claim be good,
The Nevils are thy subjects to command.
YORK: Then thus:
Edward the Third, my lords, had seven sons:
The first, Edward the Black Prince, Prince of Wales;
The second, William of Hatfield; and the third,
Lionel, Duke of Clarence; next to whom
Was John of Gaunt, the Duke of Lancaster;
The fifth was Edmund Langley, Duke of York;
The sixth was Thomas of Woodstock, Duke of Gloucester;
William of Windsor was the seventh and last.
Edward the Black Prince died before his father,
And left behind him Richard, his only son,
Who after Edward the Third's death, reign'd as king,
Till Henry Bolingbroke, Duke of Lancaster,
The eldest son and heir of John of Gaunt,
Crowned by the name of Henry the Fourth,
Seized on the realm, deposed the rightful King,
Sent his poor Queen to France, from whence she came,
And him to Pomfret, where, as all you know,
Harmless Richard was murdered traitorously.
WAR.: Father, the Duke hath told the truth;
Thus got the house of Lancaster the crown.
YORK: Which now they hold by force, and not by right;
For Richard, the first son's heir, being dead,
The issue of the next son should have reigned.
SAL.: But William of Hatfield died without an heir.
YORK: The third son, Duke of Clarence, from whose line
I claim the crown, had issue, Philip, a daughter,
Who married Edmund Mortimer, Earl of March;
Edmund had issue, Roger, Earl of March;
Roger had issue, Edmund, Anne, and Eleanor.
SAL.: This Edmund, in the reign of Bolingbroke,
As I have read, laid claim unto the crown;
And but for Owen Glendower, had been King,
Who kept him in captivity till he died.
But to the rest.
YORK: His eldest sister, Anne,
My mother, being heir unto the crown,
Married Richard Earl of Cambridge, who was
To Edmund Langley, Edward the Third's fifth son, son.
By her I claim the Kingdom. She was heir
To Roger Earl of March, who was the son
Of Edmund Mortimer; who married Philip,

> Sole daughter unto Lionel Duke of Clarence.
> So, if the issue of the elder son
> Succeed before the younger, I am King.

This is a long passage, but it is as lucid and succinct as any attempt to paraphrase the complicated relationships. Though here, as in *2 Henry IV*, and in the sources that Shakespeare followed, the second Edmund Mortimer (who was fifth Earl of March, and heir-designate to the throne of Richard II when his father died in 1398) is confused – or conflated – with his uncle, also Edmund Mortimer, but never Earl of March, the younger brother of Roger Earl of March.

The grand theme of Shakespeare's history plays is the emergence of a unified nation from the protracted civil wars of the fifteenth century. Back behind that period is imagined an idealised medieval world of order and ceremony, divinely sanctioned and approved. This ideal world was destroyed by Henry Bolingbroke's usurpation and the murder of Richard II, though it had already been endangered by Richard's own follies and crimes. There might be intervals of success and glory—as in the reign of Henry V—but that crime of rebellion against the true king, tantamount to sacrilege, since the king was God's representative on earth, had to be atoned for. The Bishop of Carlisle at the time of Richard's deposition prophesies the disasters to follow:

> And shall the figure of God's majesty,
> His captain, steward, deputy elect,
> Anointed, crowned, planted many years,
> Be judg'd by subject and inferior breath,
> And he himself not present? O forfend it, God,
> That in a Christian climate souls refin'd
> Should show so heinous, black, obscene a deed!
> I speak to subjects, and a subject speaks,
> Stirr'd up by God thus boldly for his king.
> My Lord of Herford here, whom you call king,
> Is a foul traitor to proud Herford's king,
> And if you crown him, let me prophesy—
> The blood of English shall manure the ground,
> And future ages groan for this foul act,
> Peace shall go sleep with Turks and infidels,
> And, in this seat of peace, tumultuous wars
> Shall kin with kin, and kind with kind, confound.
> Disorder, horror, fear, and mutiny,
> Shall here inhabit, and this land be call'd
> The field of Golgotha and dead men's skulls—
> O, if you raise this house against this house,
> It will the woefullest division prove
> That ever fell upon this cursed earth.   (*Richard II*, IV.1.125–47)

The view encouraged by the Tudors was that the evil let loose in England by the deposition and murder of Richard II came to some kind of culmination in Richard III. With his death the curse was cleared, and Richmond, as Henry VII, could reunite the warring factions by his marriage to Elizabeth, the surviving Yorkist princess, daughter of Edward IV. Richmond, as a Lancastrian, claimed descent from John of Gaunt through the Earl of Somerset, younger brother of Henry IV. This claim was a little distant, but it was not subject to close scrutiny. Richmond also claimed Katherine of Valois as his grandmother—she had married Owen Tudor after the death of Henry V, her first husband. And Owen Tudor, though a fairly obscure Welsh gentleman, had the distinction of being descended from the legendary King Arthur, King of Britain and lord of the famous 'Round Table' of noble knights. Because of this connection Henry VII's eldest son was christened Arthur. It was unfortunate that he died after his betrothal to Katherine of Aragon, but before the marriage. So valuable a political match could not be wasted, so Katherine was married to the younger brother, Prince Henry, later Henry VIII. His marital problems faced England with further dynastic difficulties. Three of his six wives had each one child. He was succeeded first by the youngest, Edward VI, son of Jane Seymour, then by the eldest, Mary, daughter of Katherine of Aragon and wife of King Philip of Spain, and finally by Elizabeth, the middle child, daughter of Anne Boleyn. None of these children had children of their own. When Shakespeare wrote *1 Henry IV*—probably around 1596 or 1597—Queen Elizabeth was over sixty, and resolutely refused to nominate her heir. It is no wonder that questions of legitimacy and succession should have exercised her subjects' minds. Lady Jane Grey—a granddaughter of Henry VII—had been executed in 1554 because powerful relatives had tried to place her on the throne after the death of Edward VI, but the supporters of Mary had proved more powerful. Lady Jane was descended from Henry VII's younger sister, Mary. The elder sister, Margaret, had been married to James IV, King of Scotland. Her granddaughter, Mary Queen of Scots, who had been betrothed (at six years old) to the heir to the throne of France, had married him ten years later and been widowed two years after that, had claimed the title of Queen of England in 1559. A consequence was her execution by a reluctant Elizabeth in 1587. Mary's son, James VI of Scotland, succeeded Elizabeth as James I of England, and he had the strongest dynastic claim, but there were others, and there were besides powerful, un- scrupulous and foolhardy men ready to attempt to use a power vacuum for their own advantage, as the abortive Essex rebellion of 1601 showed. There was a good deal of contemporary cogency to the general moral of the illegitimacy and disastrous consequences of any act of rebellion against established authority. Such views were widely propagated during Elizabeth's reign.

It is a possible view that when Shakespeare began his great historical work he accepted without too much question the official 'Tudor myth' view of providential history as it is found in Hall's *Chronicle*. The *Henry VI* plays are generally assumed to be among his earliest work for the theatre. It used to be argued that these plays were his apprentice revisions of work by other hands, though this is no longer widely believed. It is clear though that such a reading of the 'second tetralogy' (*Richard II, 1 Henry IV, 2 Henry IV,* and *Henry V*) would be a considerable over-simplification. These plays, which were probably written between 1595 and 1599, are much more assured and mature, and much more intellectually sophisticated work than the 'first tetralogy'. It is not that there is anything in them which explicitly contradicts official views—as, for example, does Marlowe's *Tamburlane*, the story of a shepherd who rises to be emperor of most of the world. Such views, although contained within these plays, seem limited and shallow when offered as explanations: politics and history cannot be cramped into such easy patterns.

Shakespeare began writing his epic sequence of dramas in the middle, with the death of the great Lancastrian king, Henry V. He completed the sequence to the accession of the first of the Tudors, Henry VII. Then, after a pause during which he probably wrote the early comedies and *King John*, he returned to the beginning with *Richard II* and followed through to a conclusion with Henry V's victorious wars in France. The Bishop of Carlisle's prophecy—quoted above from *Richard II*—foretells the disasters to follow, and the epilogue to *Henry V* refers explicitly to the plays already written:

> Small time, but in that small most greatly liv'd
> This star of England: Fortune made his sword,
> By which the world's best garden he achiev'd,
> And of it left his son imperial lord.
> Henry the Sixth, in infant bands crown'd King
> Of France and England, did this king succeed;
> Whose state so many had the managing,
> That they lost France and made his England bleed:
> Which oft our stage hath shown ...

The effect of thus ending and beginning in the middle is curiously equivocal, and gives a sense of history's recurrences. This is enhanced by the contrasts and parallels between the two tetralogies. Richard II, like Henry VI, came to the throne in infancy, and grew up under the control of a group of powerful nobles. Both kings, when they came of age and took charge of their own affairs, proved incompetent, but in different ways. Richard, the 'true' king, whose claim to the throne was never questioned, proved irresponsible, selfish and extravagant; he ruled through favourites, squandered money and imposed excessive taxes, and was responsible for the murder of one of his uncles. Henry VI by contrast was a saintly incompetent, trusting, gullible, easily dominated, but in principle at least honest, just, and deeply pious. A similar contrast and comparison can be made between the kings who end the two sequences, Henry V and Richard III. Both are men of outstanding ability as soldiers and politicians and both are capable of deep guile and dissimulation. But one is an arch-villain and is destroyed, and the other a national hero, the conqueror of France. Theatre audiences, on the whole, enjoy and empathise with Richard III's conscious delight in his own villainy, while Henry V—particularly when he is still Prince Hal in the Henry IV plays—is found to be a cold fish, not nearly so likeable as Falstaff, whom he rejects, or Hotspur, whom he kills.

Another way of assessing the difference between the two sets of four plays in terms of their attitudes and ideological content would be to say that the later tetralogy—that concerned with the earlier period of history—is approaching a tragic view of life. The providential view of history that is found in Edward Hall cannot be tragic. God's direct intervention in human affairs, punishing sin, causing evil to work itself out, and re-establishing the correct order of society, provides comedy in the sense of the *Divina Commedia* by Dante Alighieri (1265–1321) or *Paradise Lost*, the epic poem by John Milton (1608–74); evil is ultimately self-defeating and in the end only produces greater good. At the same time, men are reduced to instrumental status by the nature of God's purposes and the fact of his intervention. If the innocent appear to suffer—as so obviously they do in the incessant battles of the *Henry VI* plays—then this suffering is temporary and apparent only, all to be redressed by some higher tribunal. This supernatural power is manifest at the end of *Richard III* in the troop of ghosts which bless Richmond and curse Richard before the battle of Bosworth Field.

In the second tetralogy the sacramental nature of kingship is still asserted, but the world in which divinely appointed kings have to rule is a very practical and material one. Richard II is correct when he says:

Not all the water in the rough rude sea
Can wash the balm off from an anointed king;
                                        (*Richard II*, III.2.54–5)

but it does not follow from this that the anointed king, as mortal, cannot be deposed, humiliated and finally murdered. The sacramental metaphors of Richard's kingship cannot be interpreted as literal truths. As the Bishop of Carlisle—who later prophesies the disasters to follow Richard's deposition—tells him:

The means that heaven yields must be imbrac'd
And not neglected.   (*Richard II*, III.2.29–30)

Richard must act, practically and decisively—and he fails. Richard's deposition and murder are criminal and sacrilegious acts, and merit divine displeasure, and the disasters which the Bishop of Carlisle prophesies come to pass; but the events which are presented in the two parts of *Henry IV* and in *Henry V* are events in a natural world of cause and effect. The rebellions against Henry IV are the consequence of his own weak title to the crown and the loyalties, envies and ambitions of other men. As Macbeth realises, contemplating his murder of an anointed king in a later play:

> we but teach
> Bloody instructions, which, being taught, return
> To plague th' inventor.
>
> > (*Macbeth*, I.7.8–10)

Henry IV has moments of remorse, and knows his guilt:

> God knows, my son,
> By what by-paths and indirect crook'd ways
> I met this crown ...
>
> > (*2 Henry IV*, IV.5.183–5)

But even on his deathbed his advice and his motives seem pragmatic. Even the intention of a crusade, which might have seemed an act of penance, had a political motive.

> I ... had a purpose now
> To lead out many to the Holy Land,
> Lest rest and lying still might make them look
> Too near unto my state. Therefore, my Harry,
> Be it thy course to busy giddy minds
> With foreign quarrels.
>
> > (*2 Henry IV*, IV.5.209–14)

The heroic wars of *Henry V* look rather different in the light of that advice. Henry V has his own misgivings at moments of crisis also, most notably on the eve of the battle of Agincourt:

> Not today, O Lord!
> O not today, think not upon the fault
> My father made in compassing the crown!
> I Richard's body have interred new,
> And on it have bestow'd more contrite tears
> Than from it issued forced drops of blood.
> Five hundred poor I have in yearly pay,
> Who twice a day their wither'd hands hold up
> Toward heaven, to pardon blood; and I have built

Two chantries, where the sad and solemn priests
Sing still for Richard's soul. More will I do;
Though all that I can do is nothing worth,
Since that my penitence comes after all,
Imploring pardon.
(*Henry V*, IV.1.298–311)

Even at this point there is an impression of the politician about Henry; he might even be thought to be attempting to bribe the Almighty by enumerating the material extent of his penitence. Only at the very end does he seem to glimpse what is a painfully clear dilemma for Claudius, who had murdered his brother the king:

O, what form of prayer
Can serve my turn? 'Forgive me my foul murder'?
That cannot be, since I am still possess'd
Of those effects for which I did the murder:
My crown, mine own ambition, and my queen.
May one be pardon'd and retain the offence?
(*Hamlet*, III.3.51–6)

Quotations from the tragedies have been used to make explicit ideas which are implicit in the later history plays: the inevitable consequences of acts in the natural world and the irrelevance of pious intentions. Henry V wins the battle at Agincourt and with proper (and politic) piety attributes it to the Lord: 'Take it, God, For it is none but thine!' (IV.8.111–12). But we have been clearly shown the overweening incompetence of the French high command. If both Henry IV and Henry V sometimes have qualms of conscience about how they came to the throne, they have in practice no option except to maintain their own power and authority. This is not simply a matter of self-protection, it is also a matter of good government and national welfare. It is perfectly clear that the alternatives to the strong government of the usurper Henry IV are something much worse: the plan to divide the kingdom and the pointless squabbles over trivia in III.1. in *1 Henry IV* demonstrate this. Politics has been defined as the 'art of the possible' – and this usually involves compromise and the sacrifice of principle. Brutus, in Shakespeare's *Julius Caesar*, is persuaded to murder his friend Caesar for what he takes to be the best of old-fashioned republican political principles. The consequences are disastrous: civil war, and the rule of the triumvirate, which is far more authoritarian and arbitrary than Caesar at his worst. The two parts of *Henry IV* and *Henry V* are sometimes said to be Shakespeare's version of that common Renaissance theme, the 'education' of the ideal ruler. If so, the process is not an easy one and the result is a long way from that product of the popular imagination shown in the earlier play (which was known to Shakespeare) *The Famous Victories of Henry V*. Henry is not the happy warrior with the common touch there displayed, but a cold and deeply devious man – and it is exactly his commitment to the welfare of his country that makes him this. The history plays approach a tragic view of life, because they convey a sense of the human cost to Prince Henry himself—and not to him alone—of his decision to become a responsible king. In *3 Henry VI*, II.5, at the battle of Towton, Henry VI sits down on a molehill as the battle rages and compares the happy state of shepherds with the cares and miseries of kingship. Two pairs of opposing soldiers from the battle come into his view: one a son who has just killed his father, the other a father who has killed his own son. Their grief, and the king's, as they discover the identity of their opponents, is symbolic of the miseries of civil war. It is deeply pathetic, but it is *not* tragic just because it *is* symbolic, because it is shown as the operation of general causes. This is what civil war is like, what it leads to, but the persons are not known to us. We have not seen the particular choices that brought these sons and fathers to opposing sides in this particular battle. It is possible to see the king Prince Henry becomes as the consequence of the choice Prince Henry makes—the choice, in effect, to become king. He must accept the consequences of that choice even though they may be unpleasant and may turn him into a kind of person he might not wish to be. Providential history does not allow human freedom. Tragedy does, but it is a limited freedom, and its limitation is exactly the unavoidable consequences of our freely chosen actions.

1 Henry IV as a history play

It is clear that Percy's defeat at the battle of Shrewsbury is the triumph of the Prince, and that we have been moving towards this reversal of reputations from that initial unflattering comparison made between the two by the King in I.1. Harry Hotspur is revealed as the play goes on as hot-tempered, naïve and easily manipulated by such politicians as his uncle Worcester; positively irresponsible in his attitudes to the welfare of the country as a whole; and his sense of honour appears largely a matter of self-esteem. While there is no question of his qualities as a warrior, or even as a commander in the field, the dialogue at the council of war before the battle of Shrewsbury may indicate that he is not a very good strategist. He remains an attractive person, though, for his energy and cheerfulness, and the fine flow of his language, and not least for the joking, and clearly affectionate, relationship with his wife.

Both the popular and chronicle sources provided Shakespeare with the story of a prince who underwent an abrupt and radical transformation of character when he became king. The problem for the dramatist, looking forward (we may be fairly certain) to the completion of his scheme of a linked sequence of plays on English history, was to find some way of making that remarkable conversion psychologically and dramatically convincing, while at the same time presenting the popular legendary material about the wild youth. He does this in two ways: one is by simply soft-pedalling the disorderly episodes. The highway robbery is converted into a practical joke against the robbers, and the Prince refuses to take part before Poins makes this proposal to him. We are reassured at the end that the money taken is repaid. The legendary episode of Prince Henry striking the Chief Justice a blow on the ear and being sent to prison for it gets a passing mention in *2 Henry IV*, I.2.193, and at V.2.73–101 the Chief Justice justifies his action. In *Richard II* Prince Henry, 'young wanton, and effeminate boy', as his father describes him, proposed to go:

> unto the stews,
> And from the common'st creature pluck a glove,
> And wear it as a favour; and with that
> He would unhorse the lustiest challenger.
> *(Richard II, V.3.16–19)*

This, according to Hotspur in that play, was his response to the proposal of a tournament at Oxford in celebration of his father's accession. But there is no hint of sexual impropriety in the later plays. The other method by which the transformation of the 'madcap prince' into the great king is prepared, is in making him explain his excursions into the low life of London as an act of conscious choice and policy.

> So when this loose behaviour I throw off,
> And pay the debt I never promised,
> By how much better than my word I am,
> By so much shall I falsify men's hopes;
> And like bright metal on a sullen ground,
> My reformation, glitt'ring o'er my fault,
> Shall show more goodly, and attract more eyes
> Than that which hath no foil to set it off.
> I'll so offend, to make offence a skill,
> Redeeming time when men think least I will.
> *(I.2.203–12)*

This speech has caused a good deal of critical trouble. It is too coldly calculating for the comfort of those who wish to see the Prince as the ideal magnanimous king in preparation. So the late Professor Dover Wilson, in a very influential study, decided that it is a 'piece of dramatic convention', a soliloquy of the 'expository type' designed to convey information to the audience about the general drift of the play, much as a prologue did.* But the Prince is not just informing us that 'he is determined to prove a worthy king'. He is telling us with conscious superiority that he intends to *use* these inferior creatures for his own ultimate advantage. It is not the good intention that is disturbing, but the calculation and disingenuousness that intention seems to involve. There is indeed a sardonic edge and an element of self-disgust in the Prince's wit. His alleged wildness, in fact, is transformed into something quite different—the continuous discipline of playing a role—and this is an excellent preparation for the king he becomes.

The original comparison made between Hotspur and Prince Hal is soon shown to be inadequate. Hotspur does not have all the virtues he is supposed to have and Hal is not as black as he is painted. His 'wildness' (unlike Hotspur's) is a conscious role and he does not do anything vicious. In the scene of reconciliation with his father (where it appears that King Henry's objections to his son's behaviour are as much to its being impolitic as to its immorality), the Prince claims:

Percy is but my factor, good my lord,
To engross up glorious deeds on my behalf,
And I will call him to so strict account
That he shall render every glory up,
Yea, even the slightest worship of his time,
Or I will tear the reckoning from his heart.
                                        (III.2.147–52)

However, though the play ends with Percy defeated, its action is not a simple reversal, with Hal and Hotspur changing places. For one thing, the Prince does not get the public credit for the death of Hotspur: that is claimed by Falstaff, and Hal undertakes to 'gild [his lie] with the happiest terms I have' (V.5.157). At one level of understanding this act raises the Prince in the esteem of the audience, but it cannot do this for the other characters in the play, since they know nothing of it. Since Falstaff gains a reputation for valour (as is clear from *2 Henry IV*) the opprobrium attached to his company is reduced. At a more allegorical level of interpretation it is appropriate that it is exactly his evil companion, the devil that haunts him 'in the likeness of an old fat man' (II.4.441) that prevents him from getting the full credit for his actions at Shrewsbury.

Besides this, though, what has taken place is an adjustment of values, not just a change of roles. We are shown—not least by Falstaff's 'catechism' at the end of V.1.—that the Hotspur view of honour is a very limited one. Hotspur is too well bred to say himself 'I'm the greatest!', but when Douglas says 'Thou art the king of honour' (IV.1.10) he does not deny the praise. His idea of honour (like a reckless adolescent's)

*John Dover Wilson, *The Fortunes of Falstaff*, Cambridge University Press, Cambridge, 1943, p.41.

involves doing dangerous things, but it also involves public recognition for that doing. King Henry begins his interview with Prince Hal by attacking:

> such inordinate and low desires,
> Such poor, such bare, such lewd, such mean attempts,
> Such barren pleasures, rude society
>
> (III.2.12–14)

But he moves quickly and with increasing vehemence to the Prince's public reputation. He contrasts his own reserved and dignified demeanour when a young man with that of King Richard, 'The skipping King, he ambled up and down', and concludes 'For all the world/As thou art to this hour was Richard then'. Again Hotspur is brought into the comparison: Hotspur is the Henry Bolingbroke to Prince Hal's Richard. This is ironic, since by this point in the play the audience ought to be more aware than King Henry is of the Prince's virtues and Hotspur's limitations. For Hotspur 'honour'—which might, with good Shakespearean precedent, be called 'reputation'—is an end in itself, and brave deeds are the means to that end. For King Henry reputation is itself a means to a further end: the gaining and keeping of power. Falstaff calls honour 'a mere scutcheon' (V.1.140), and says he'll none of it; all the same his opportunism in claiming credit for Hotspur's death shows that he is perfectly willing to exploit it for his own advantage. This cynicism undermines both Hotspur's heroics and the King's prudential wisdom. The Prince's first soliloquy has shown us that he is as much aware as his father of the value of reputation. He is applying this knowledge in a long-term strategy which will use his present bad reputation to enhance his future good reputation: 'I'll so offend to make offence a skill'. This suggests a political acumen even profounder and more devious than his father's. At the same time, when he allows Falstaff the credit for Hotspur's death he shows that he has no personal need for the outward recognition that matters so much to Hotspur, who would 'wear / Without corrival all [honour's] dignities'. In the context of the two-part play—and the two parts of *Henry IV* are more closely related than any other pair of Shakespeare's history plays—it operates as a kind of dramatic irony. It gives the spectators or readers knowledge about the Prince that no character in the play—except Falstaff—shares. It is knowledge that makes us admire the Prince for both his warlike valour and his generosity. Within the play this honour is much more limited, for Hotspur has been made Falstaff's 'factor' (III.2.147), not Hal's, and, though the Prince has done well at Shrewsbury, for those in the play he is still shadowed by a bad reputation. This clearly relates to the way in which Shakespeare has adapted the legend from his sources of the wild youth suddenly transformed into the model king. Hal's combat with

Hotspur has no historical basis, though 'the Prince that daie holpe his father like a lustie yoong gentleman' according to Holinshed's *Chronicle*. The fiction that Falstaff took the credit is possible because no individual is named in the sources as responsible for Hotspur's death. By the battle of Shrewsbury Shakespeare's Prince Hal is already much nearer to reformation than his contemporaries can know. His excursion into low life is an act of political wisdom beyond the scope of his father. If initially a natural predilection it has become an assumed role. He may enjoy the role, but he is fully aware that it must be rejected. Hotspur, at first presented as the ideal young warrior, is shown to be dangerously irresponsible. While the Prince *plays* at a robbery (the money taken will be returned) Hotspur prepares to steal a third of the kingdom. The Prince, in spite of his reputation for levity, proves a better soldier than Hotspur and defeats him in heroic single combat and then, in marked contrast to Hotspur, is so unconcerned about his own reputation that he allows Falstaff to take all the credit for this act. Here it seems we have the ideal prince: in spite of appearances he is politically wise and responsible, less concerned than his father with outward shows; a valiant warrior but so modest and magnanimous that he lets another man take all the credit.

By the end of the play, then, we have a very different view of the major characters and of their motives and values from that which we had at the beginning. The expected things have been shown: on the moral and political level the defeat of rebels who are wicked enough to plan the division of the country, but at the same time the guilt and uneasiness of the usurping yet successful Henry IV. On a more personal level the attractive bravado and masculinity of Harry Hotspur, the scheming of the envious Worcester, and, most importantly, the roistering of the wild young Prince and his companions have been presented. In its own day *1 Henry IV* was probably Shakespeare's most popular play, and no doubt a large part of the attraction was the invention of Falstaff. But while meeting expectations at one level *1 Henry IV* may also raise doubts at another. They may lead to the conclusion that the requirements of kingship, for which the Prince is training himself, are complex, difficult and perhaps even damaging for the man who has to meet them.

After the battle of Shrewsbury Prince Henry delivers Douglas 'ransomless and free' (V.5.28). This is a chivalrous and magnanimous action, and yet it can produce a certain uneasiness, especially if it is remembered that it is very close to the political advice of Worcester to Hotspur in I.3. It is not that Prince Henry is not magnanimous; it is the suspicion that even his most magnanimous acts have a covert political motive that is disturbing.

It is perhaps in his relations with Falstaff that the Prince's cold and calculating nature appears most clearly. Falstaff is a brilliant and much admired dramatic character, the 'part' for an actor which dominates both plays, but what he represents is a kind of man that most of us, in real life, would take great pains to avoid (a distinction that many critics of the play seem to forget). Falstaff is a drunkard, a lecher, a thief, a gross bohemian who lives by his wits and by exploiting his charm. He is quite without scruple regarding the property, the reputation or even the lives of others, where he sees his own advantage, and this is demonstrated again and again in the two parts of *Henry IV*. It is only because he lives in an immediate world of appetites to be satisfied and dangers to be avoided, and shows little sign of 'looking before and after' that he is not more destructive. Despite his wit, intelligence and huge vitality, he is a great baby, the unmoral infant in each one of us, that seeks the gratification of every desire as soon as it is felt—because there is no other time but *now*.

The great contrast to Falstaff is the King in this regard. For King Henry the present is a usually unwelcome intrusion and obstruction of an ideal future, the time when plots and rebellions will at last be over, when he will be secure on his throne, with a dutiful son preparing to succeed him, and can at last perform the act of penance that will make things right even with God, his expedition to Jerusalem. This emerges in the King's first speech in the first scene of the play. The irrelevance of time to Falstaff is the basis of his first bout of wit with Prince Hal at the opening of the second scene of the play.

Falstaff is a consistent user and misleader of others. He prays on their good nature, their gullibility and their weaknesses; as a highway robber he preys directly—and it is clear that he, Gadshill, Poins and the others are regular thieves. 'Why, Hal, 'tis my vocation, Hal,' he says at I.2.101. He thinks that he is using the Prince, whether to pay the bill, to protect him from the law ('we steal as in a castle, cock-sure' says Gadshill (II.1.85)) or to give him the credit for killing Hotspur. At the end of *2 Henry IV* the Prince, coming from his coronation as King Henry V, coldly rejects Falstaff.

I know thee not, old man. Fall to thy prayers.
How ill white hairs become a fool and jester!
I have long dreamt of such a kind of man,
So surfeit-swell'd, so old, and so profane;
But being awak'd I do despise my dream.
(V.5.47–51)

There has been a long critical debate about the morality and the acceptability in dramatic terms of this rejection. Perhaps part of the uneasiness to which the rejection of Falstaff gives rise comes from the sense that he himself has been outwitted; that he has been used, consistently and with forethought, over a long period by the machiavellian Prince. There is an element of truth in Falstaff's complaint:

> Thou hast done much harm upon me, Hal, God forgive thee for it:
> before I knew thee, Hal, I knew nothing, and now am I, if a man
> should speak truly, little better than one of the wicked ...
>
> (I.2.89—92)

This is a typically Falstaffian exaggeration, but there seems little doubt
that the Prince's countenance and credit have enlarged the scope of
Falstaff's activities considerably. Shakespeare's later history plays
modified the orthodox Tudor view of history as controlled by
Providence in the direction of a more tragic and a more humanist
understanding. This is apparent even in *1 Henry IV*, which is outwardly
the most comic of these plays. The general good will almost certainly
result in some individual ill; the choice to take and use political power
may, perhaps must, result in some limiting of private virtue for the man
who, like Prince Henry, chooses it, even though his concern is for the
general good. And the loss will be in the most highly valued areas of
private life: those of inner integrity, deep friendship and mutual trust.

Part 4

Hints for study

It may be as well to begin with the very simplest advice. *1 Henry IV* is the text of a play, and it should be read as a play. To do this it may be necessary to ignore—at least to begin with—some of the material intended to help the reader that has been added to most editions of Shakespeare's plays. A play is something that happens in a limited time in a limited space—for about two and a half hours in a theatre. While a play is going on it cannot be stopped, and the member of the audience cannot, like the novel-reader, reread a passage that is not understood at once, nor refer to an earlier chapter, to remind himself about earlier events. The novel-reader can put the book down at any time and come back to it when so inclined. The theatre audience may be let out for an arbitrarily fixed interval, but that is all: and it is probable that until at least ten years after *1 Henry IV* was written plays on the Elizabethan public stages were performed continuously, like a modern film, with no break in the action from beginning to end. There are no acts and scenes marked in the quartos of *1 Henry IV*: these divisions first appear in the Folio of 1623. A novel is designed to be read at intervals over an extended period, a play to be apprehended rapidly and as a unity.

The best way to read a play is to read it continuously and complete, at a single sitting. In this way some grasp of the whole structure will be gained, and of the relation of the main parts within that structure. In a rapid reading of this kind much detail will be missed and many puzzling things will have to be left unexplained. But these can be sorted out at a second or third reading and the detail will be better understood for being seen within a frame which is already comprehended. Some important details of the play may well emerge more clearly from a rapid reading than from a slow and laborious one. The close parallel between Worcester's advice to Hotspur at I.3.225 and Prince Henry's release of Douglas without a ransom at V.5.28, or the similar nature of the imagery in the Prince's soliloquy at the end of I.2 and that of the King's reprimand in III.2.30–80 may not be consciously noticed, but is more likely to affect the reader's response if the play is read at a single sitting.

If a play is to be appreciated properly, though, it must be understood as fully as possible. If the notes and glossaries are ignored on a first reading they must be attended to later. To start with, the elucidation of obscure passages in the text of the play will be like the translation of a foreign language. Concepts not available in modern English will be paraphrased, and information which Shakespeare and his audience took for granted, but which we do not have, will be provided. With increasing familiarity with the play a lot of this material is assimilated, and so more is understood, and understood more fully. Again, the analogy with learning a foreign language is useful. There comes a point in learning a language when it is no longer necessary to translate in order to understand. When that happens the learner has really begun to know the language. So the reader of Shakespeare who no longer needs to keep consulting the notes has really begun to understand the play. The aim of study should be this capacity to read the play rapidly with ready comprehension. A play should at first be read straight through, but after that must come the detailed study, until an informed reading of the play is possible.

The text of a play, it should always be remembered, is not, like a novel, designed primarily for the private reader. The text of a play is like the score of a piece of music: it is a guide for performance; and performances can vary. What the reader of a play must bear in mind is not so much what the possible 'real' situation that is being represented might be, but what the stage situation would be, how it would be organised, and how it would be understood. There are many scenes, for example, where the presence of silent characters can be very significant. In Shakespeare's *Richard II* the first scene of Act IV, the scene of Richard's deposition, is a most important scene—so much so that the last one hundred and fifty lines of it were censored during Elizabeth I's reign as politically dangerous. In that scene Henry Bolingbroke—Henry IV—says very little and other characters, particularly King Richard II, say a great deal, but it is Henry who dominates and controls everything that goes on. The reader who forgets this powerful presence in the long passages when he is silent will not fully understand the scene. The play in performance would find visual means to make Henry Bolingbroke's dominance apparent. There are, perhaps, no instances in *1 Henry IV* as significant as this, but there are several where it is worth considering what a silent character is doing, how he is reacting to what is going on. Worcester, for example, is on stage for the whole of III.1, and yet he has only two speeches, and only one (ll.171–83), when he reprimands Hotspur for his behaviour towards Glendower, of any significance. How is he responding to what the other characters say and do while he is silently present? In the next scene, III.2, only the King and the Prince are present. Through most of the scene the Prince is silent, while the King lectures him on his bad behaviour. How does the Prince react? Is he resentful? Is he bored? Is he genuinely repentant? Does he pretend to be repentant? Is he only provoked to speech at last by the King's suggestion that he will go over to the rebel side himself, or has he been trying to get a word in for some time without being able to break the flow of the King's rhetoric? These questions are left as questions because, while some answers may be more likely than others, there is no single absolutely clear answer. There are different ways of playing the scene.

This possible range of interpretation of a play in performance (any one performance can, of course, present only one interpretation: a performance must be consistent with itself) relates to the problem of character in Shakespeare's plays. In 1777 Maurice Morgan wrote his *Essay on the Dramatic Character of Sir John Falstaff* in which he argued that Falstaff was not a coward. This, at the time, was almost a paradox, in direct contradiction of the view of the greatest critic of that age, Samuel Johnson, but later on it came to be widely accepted, and it is still an issue that can be debated. This is not an indication that Shakespeare's presentation of the character is confused or inconsistent. It is rather that it is rich and complex. Our understanding of character is complicated by the fact that words and values shift over long periods of time. In the days when British power was great—say from the middle of the nineteenth century to the world war that ended in 1945—it was common to see Shakespeare's history plays—and particularly the four that culminate in Henry V's conquest of France—as patriotic celebrations of emerging national greatness. So no doubt they were, but more recent events have made us more sensitive to the elements of cold political realism that are also there. This in its turn changes our response to other characters in the play, as well as to Falstaff. The issue of character is never simple: any one character is always seen in the context of others, and all are seen—like the whole play—coloured by the particular needs and presuppositions that any age brings with it. If, for example, we take a fairly 'modern' view of Prince Henry, a view that stresses his cold political intelligence, his full consciousness, from the soliloquy that ends I.2 onwards, of what he is doing, and the ends he has in view in doing it, how does this affect our understanding of Falstaff? Do we then see in Falstaff more of the good-natured merrymaker, the fertile wit, the man who enjoys life's fleeting moments as they come? Such a Falstaff would be almost a victim of the Prince's calculating nature, his humanity would contrast favourably with the rigid and inhibited nature of the Prince, none of whose acts are spontaneous but all directed to some ulterior end. A more traditional view of the Prince plays down or is embarrassed by the soliloquy (as in Dover Wilson's account quoted on pp.77–8) and puts more responsibility on Falstaff for the Prince's wild behaviour. Or again, a 'political' Prince might be combined with an interpretation of Falstaff that stressed his unscrupulousness and cynicism. Such a Falstaff would himself be a calculating person, playing the fool to please the Prince with an eye always to his own long-term advantage. 'Sweet wag, when thou art king ...' (I.2.23) would have a sinister resonance, then, and the audience would be left in no doubt about the fate of those ragamuffins Falstaff had led 'where they are peppered' (V.3.36). Such an interpretation of the play would be a very dark one, a long way from the patriotic celebration that used to be in fashion.

The discussion of character is probably the commonest as well as the most traditional way of talking about Shakespeare's plays, but it is not the only way. We can think of the action of the play—its 'story'—as able to be understood at various levels of abstraction. One of the stage traditions that lies behind Shakespeare's plays, as E. M. W. Tillyard makes clear (see Part 5, Suggestions for further reading), is the moral allegory, where characters are types, or stand for virtues and vices and other human attributes. This tradition was still active in Shakespeare's time, and he refers to it at II.4.447–9: 'that reverend Vice, that grey Iniquity, that Father Ruffian, that Vanity in years'. All the words given capital initials could be the names or titles of characters from these plays. A frequent theme of these plays was the parable of the Prodigal Son (Falstaff refers to it at IV.2.34–6). A young man, tempted by those things to which youth is prone—drink, lechery, gambling—falls into bad company and bad ways, may be condemned to death for a crime and—much worse, of course, in this Christian moral allegory—may be in danger of eternal damnation. If he is saved, it is by Good Counsel and God's Grace. Clearly, the Prince's relation with Falstaff can be fitted to this pattern. In *Henry V* his reformation is explained in terms of divine grace by the Archbishop of Canterbury:

> Consideration like an angel came
> and whipp'd th' offending Adam out of him,
> Leaving his body as a Paradise,
> T'envelop and contain celestial spirits.   (I.1.28–31)

The simple moral allegory was extended to political themes, and here would focus on the nature of good government and the kind of person who made a good ruler. The Prodigal Son story became the Education of the Prince—for princes, having great power, are subject to greater temptation than ordinary men. Here Falstaff's role—allegorically presented in his name, false staff—as the misleader and bad councillor is clear; Hotspur can be seen as a model of what the Prince should be—King Henry makes this explicit in I.1.77–89—and the welfare of the whole community depends on the outcome. When Gadshill is explaining to Chamberlain that he is safe because he robs in good company, he makes a general point about the hypocrisy of the powerful:

> ... they pray continually to their saint the
> commonwealth, or rather not pray to her, but
> prey on her, for they ride up and down on her,
> and make her their boots.   (II.1.78–81)

But as well as being, at this simple level, a political morality, *1 Henry IV* is a history play: general conclusions may be drawn from it, but it is about particular events. It is not, however, a simple objective recapitulation of the events—if that were possible. It is a treatment of the events that is already moralised. The history of the Wars of the Roses, the events that led up to the foundation of the Tudor dynasty in England, were of great interest and were much discussed (see p.68 above). There was an established view of what had happened, and of how it was to be understood. Henry IV has to be both a strong and able ruler and a guilty and remorse-ridden man; the Prince has to be first a wild and outrageous youth, but is later destined to be a great king and national hero; the rebels are courageous and good soldiers, and not without some cause for their discontent, but they are basically self-interested and lacking in political responsibility. The unity and welfare of England is not—as it is with Henry IV, and even more with his son—their main concern.

All these different frameworks underlie Shakespeare's treatment of his characters. These are the restrictions within which he had to work, and against which he must establish the humanity, the psychological reality of his characters. If Shakespeare had reservations about the official interpretation of the history with which he was dealing—and he may have had—those reservations had still to be communicated through, and not against, the expectations his audience had about certain episodes and interpretations, and his characterisation must still be compatible. As we move from the simplest level of moral allegory to the complexities of character-in-action, at each level a more inclusive understanding of the play emerges, and some modification of the view is required. Most of us look for simple explanations, as far as possible, and there is a tendency, particularly in matters of politics or patriotism, to see things in black and white, as simple conflicts of the good (our lot) and the bad. A reading of *1 Henry IV* that ends up with a simple polarity of right versus wrong will be a very limited one.

There are two other ways in which a Shakespeare play may be usefully considered: first as a dramatic poem and secondly as a sequence of scenes. In each case a much higher degree of conscious attention is paid to one particular aspect of the play than would be possible in the theatre situation. The understanding that can be gained by these means, though, can be applied back to the performance or reading of the play, deepening our appreciation and, perhaps, making us aware of why we respond in the way we do to certain passages.

If we consider *1 Henry IV* as a dramatic poem we consider it as a construction of language. When we talk about the characters in a play we are, in a way, going through the language to what the language conveys. All the primary evidence anyone has about Falstaff or Henry IV is the words Shakespeare puts into their mouths, and into the mouths of other people about them. When Hotspur says 'I . . . have not well the gift of tongue' (V.2.77), we do not believe him. We have heard his passionate rhetoric in I.3, and his sarcastic wit in III.1; his words have already given us a character of whom that statement (although Hotspur may be perfectly sincere in making it) is false.

The term 'dramatic poem' has been used in spite of the fact that a large proportion of this play is written in prose. It is clear, all the same, that there is nothing haphazard about the change from one to the other. Some characters speak verse all the time: the King and most of the nobility. Others speak prose throughout: Falstaff and most of the humble people. Others alternate from one to the other: Hotspur and, most significantly, the Prince. The listener in the theatre may not consciously note 'aha! now the Prince has started talking poetry'—but he will certainly respond to the elevation of tone, the greater formality, the stronger rhythmic effect of verse. There is a decorum, a 'rightness', in these changes. In I.2 the Prince with his low companions speaks prose, but at the end of the scene, left alone, he becomes himself, and speaks as a prince should, in elevated verse. In III.1, towards the end, when Glendower's daughter sings a song in Welsh, Hotspur's impatience is demonstrated by his asides and innuendoes to his wife (ll.221–30). The rhythms 'wander in the no-man's land between prose and verse' (as A. R. Humphreys remarks in the Arden edition) but after the song (ll.238 ff.) become much more clearly prose, emphasising Hotspur's separation from the other characters. In V.4, when Falstaff has given his account (in prose) of how he killed Hostspur, Prince John remarks, 'This is the strangest tale that ever I heard' (l.153). This is a prosaic enough remark, but it happens also to be a reasonably regular blank-verse line and it makes a bridge to Prince Henry's verse speech which follows.

Shakespeare's verse is capable of a great deal of variety. Although basically of a five-stressed ten-syllable line it is by no means rigid. Extra unstressed syllables and shifts in the stress are common. In any case since there are (as phoneticians tell us) at least four levels of stress in use in English and stress is relative within the foot, many subtle variations are possible. The verse can encompass the high style in which Vernon describes Prince Henry and his companions (IV.1.97–110) or the rapid angry exchange between Hotspur and Glendower at III.1.108–21, where a number of the lines of verse are shared between two speakers. There is a comparable range of style available in prose, from the parody of an old-fashioned ornate rhetoric when Falstaff plays the King (II.4.392–462) to the tavern reckoning at the end of the same scene (526–32) or the letter, counterpointed with Hotspur's angry comments, at II.3.1–35.

It is apparent that certain characters have marked individualities in their manner of speech. Falstaff is addicted to 'if-then' constructions, concluding in grotesque comparisons: 'if manhood, good manhood, be not forgot upon the face of the earth, then am I a shotten herring' (II.4.125–7), or 'If I fought not with fifty of them, I am a bunch of radish' (182–3). Hotspur, however, has an urgency of speech and lively wit that suggest strong passions and imagination.

If we look at the work as a whole then other patterns can be seen: certain kinds of image, certain kinds of comparison occur frequently, not limited to the speech of individual characters. These recurrent images or 'image clusters' as they are sometimes called, can be taken to suggest themes in the play. Attention has been drawn to the accepted parallels in 'the great chain of being' (p.19) between the political and the cosmic order. These parallels can be well illustrated from this play. There are many comparisons of royalty to the sun, of rebels to stars out of their spheres, and so on. All these emphasise the Elizabethans' need for stable order and good government.

A rather different set of comparisons is those relating to debt and commercial obligation. In one place this is explicit, not metaphorical at all:

... our indentures tripartite are drawn,
Which being sealed interchangeably,
(A business that this night may execute)
Tomorrow...

(III.1.76–9)

What the rebels are doing is a 'deal', and a rather shady deal at that, and the point is made by this use of commercial terms. Prince Henry in his soliloquy proposes to 'pay the debt I never promised' (I.2.204). Falstaff claims that the Prince owes him a thousand pounds, and when challenged responds, 'A thousand pound, Hal? A million, thy love is worth a million, thou owest me thy love (III.3.135–6).

There are many other references to debts and obligations and commercial arrangements, and they are made by a wide range of characters. There are, perhaps, two opposed implications to be drawn from this. The first is that already mentioned—that rebellion is a business, that in the end the rebels are in it for what they can get, and similar motives animate many characters. Against this there is an obligation accepted, not imposed. If society is to thrive, we must be prepared, like Prince Henry, to pay the debt that was never promised, to recognise our obligations to society. The greatest example, for a Christian society, of this acceptance of an obligation on behalf of others, is Christ himself, whose 'blessed feet':

... fourteen hundred years ago were nail'd
For our advantage on the bitter cross.

(I.1.26–7)

And 'advantage' at that time was a commercial term. Shylock, in Shakespeare's *The Merchant of Venice*, lent money 'upon advantage', which is to say he took interest on a loan.

1 Henry IV was almost certainly played without intervals in the Elizabethan theatre and there was a rapid flow on from one scene to the next. In this one respect the Elizabethan theatre was more like the cinema than the modern theatre. One of the ways in which effects are achieved in film is by the contrast or juxtaposition of one scene with another. Something like the same process is available to the Elizabethan theatre. A simple example of this in our play is the interweaving of the plotting of rebellion and the Gad's Hill robbery. The two sequences of events are quite unrelated, but by this means they become related, and rebellion is reduced from heroic stature to something like highway robbery. The comic skirmishes of II.2 anticipate the battles of V.3 and V.4. Falstaff displays his valour and discretion in both, but whereas in II.2 the Prince takes the plunder from Falstaff, in V.4 Falstaff, with his claim to have killed Hotspur, takes the prize from the Prince.

It is contrasts and comparisons of this kind that are involved in the consideration of a play as a sequence of scenes. Such contrasts and comparisons may be made more pointed in the theatre if the director arranges visual similarities in gesture, grouping or movement between one scene and another. All these different ways of considering a play—in terms of character, of varying readings of the nature of the action, as a dramatic poem and as a sequence of scenes—are partial and limited approaches. By concentrating our attention more closely on one aspect we may gain deeper understanding in that area, but these new insights must always be brought back, and combined in the most comprehensive reading of the play of which we are capable.

Questions and specimen answers

(1) Context questions

In questions of this kind a brief but significant passage from the play is quoted in the examination paper, and the candidate is asked to identify the speaker and the occasion, attach some significance to the passage and sometimes explain difficulties. In most cases there is a choice of passages from which two or three are to be selected, and each passage will be followed by three or four specific questions. Answers should be brief and to the point. Some examples follow:

Select three of the following passages,
and answer the questions which follow

(i)   So when this loose behaviour I throw off,
      And pay the debt I never promised,
      By how much better than my word I am,
      By so much shall I falsify men's hopes;
      And like bright metal on a sullen ground,
      My reformation, glitt'ring o'er my fault,
      Shall show more goodly, and attract more eyes
      Than that which hath no foil to set it off.

      (a) Who is speaking?
      (b) What is the occasion of the speech?
      (c) What does the speaker mean by 'the debt I never promised'?
      (d) What is the meaning of 'sullen ground' and 'foil'?

(ii) I will redeem all this on Percy's head,
      And in the closing of some glorious day
      Be bold to tell you that I am your son,
      When I will wear a garment all of blood,
      And stain my favours in a bloody mask,
      Which, wash'd away, shall scour my shame with it.

      (a) Who is speaking, and to whom?
      (b) What is the occasion of the speech?
      (c) What is to be redeemed on Percy's head?
      (d) What is the meaning of
                  'stain my favours in a bloody mask'?

(iii) By the Lord, our plot is a good plot, as ever was laid, our friends
      true and constant: a good plot, good friends, and full of
      expectation: an excellent plot, very good friends; what a frosty-
      spirited rogue is this! Why, my Lord of York commends the plot,
      and the general course of the action.

      (a) Who is speaking?
      (b) What is the occasion of the speech?
      (c) Is the speaker's confidence justified in the event?
      (d) Who is 'my Lord of York' and how important is his part in
           the play?

(iv) A: Come, you shall have Trent turned.
      B: I do not care, I'll give thrice so much land
          To any well-deserving friend:
          But in the way of bargain, mark ye me,
          I'll cavil on the ninth part of a hair.
          ·Are the indentures drawn? Shall we be gone?

(a) Who are A and B?

(b) What is the occasion of these speeches?

(c) For what reason had B desired to 'have Trent turned'?

(d) Explain the words 'cavil' and 'indentures'.

(v)   Lord, Lord, how this world is given to lying! I grant
you I was down, and out of breath, and so was he, but
we rose both at an instant, and fought a long hour
by Shrewsbury clock. If I may be believed, so: if not,
let them that should reward valour bear the sin
upon their own heads. I'll take it upon my death, I
gave him this wound in the thigh.

(a) Who is speaking, and to whom?

(b) What is the occasion of the speech?

(c) Who has been wounded in the thigh, and what are the
consequences?

(d) What does 'I'll take it upon my death' mean?

Answer: (The question requires only three passages to be dealt with,
though brief answers are provided here to all five)

(i) (a) Prince Henry, alone.

    (b) At the end of the second scene of the play the Prince is left
alone after jesting with Falstaff and agreeing to join in Poins's
plot to take the plunder from Falstaff and the others after
they have robbed the travellers on Gad's Hill. In this speech
the Prince reveals that his disorderly behaviour is an assumed
role. He anticipates that he will get a better reputation as a
remarkably reformed character than as a prince who is
always well behaved. The effect of contrast — 'my reformation
glitt'ring o'er my fault' — will be to his advantage.

    (c) Prince Henry recognises an obligation, as the man who will be
the next king, to serve his country. However, he has never
made any public promise to do so, and has cultivated
behaviour that suggests the reverse.

    (d) 'Sullen ground': dull background; 'foil': contrast — a thin
sheet of bright metal or black substance is set under a
precious stone to increase its lustre. This is a foil.

(ii) (a) Prince Henry is speaking to his father, the King.

    (b) The occasion is the private meeting between King and Prince
that comes in the middle of the preparations to deal with the
rebellion. This meeting has been played in jest by Falstaff and
the Prince in the main tavern scene, but the reality is very
different from that mockery. The Prince accepts his father's
reproof, and is reconciled with him when he declares his
determination to fight and defeat Hotspur.

(c) By defeating Hotspur Prince Henry will redeem his bad reputation, got by his association with Falstaff and his companions. He will gain all Percy's honour and reputation for himself. 'Percy', he tells the King, 'is but my factor'—that is, his agent.

(d) Several ideas run together in this line. 'Favours' may be either the Prince's face, or some specific identifying article of dress. Then either his face will be blood-stained in the battle, or his 'favour' will be stained with blood from other faces. In either interpretation this blood will have a purifying effect, just as, in Christian thought, Christ's blood purifies men from their sins.

(iii) (a) Hotspur is speaking alone.

(b) Hotspur is commenting as he reads a letter. It appears that someone he has approached has refused to join the rebellion because it is (in the writer's view) ill timed and badly organised, and the others involved not altogether trustworthy. Hotspur indignantly (and perhaps rashly) rejects these cautious views.

(c) Hotspur is over-confident, and secure in his own opinion even on the eve of the battle of Shrewsbury, when the letter-writer's fears are shown to be fully justified. Very few of the 'very good friends' arrive for the battle, and Hotspur is defeated and killed.

(d) 'My Lord' is the Archbishop of York, who appears only in one small scene. That scene is important, though, since it shows, before the battle, that some of those involved in the rebellion are anticipating an unsuccessful outcome. That scene also serves as a link with *2 Henry IV*, where the Archbishop of York has a much more important role.

(iv) (a) A is Glendower, B is Hotspur.

(b) The rebels, in their conference at Bangor, have agreed to divide England between them. This, in Elizabethan eyes at least, puts them very clearly in the wrong. The incipient quarrel that is ended with these speeches is a suggestion of what might follow such a division: each party would be envious of the others. Glendower gives way to Hotspur, and Hotspur promptly gives up his demand. He does 'not care', indeed; his only aim seems to be to get the better of an opponent in a confrontation. He has little sense of the responsibilities of leadership.

(c) Hotspur observes on the map a large bend in the course of the river Trent. He suggests a canal should be cut to make the river run straight, and so put the land enclosed by the bend into his territory.

(d) To 'cavil' is to argue in a hair-splitting way on trivial issues. 'Indentures' are legal documents, so called because their edges are indented where they are torn apart. These indented edges could later be matched to demonstrate the genuineness of the documents.

(v) (a) Falstaff is speaking to Prince Henry and Prince John.

(b) They have met him with Hotspur's dead body on his back, and this speech is Falstaff's response to Prince Henry's assertion that he had killed Hotspur himself and had seen Falstaff dead.

(c) Falstaff has given the corpse of Hotspur a wound in the thigh in addition to the fatal wounds Hotspur had received in his fight with Prince Henry. Falstaff can truly swear that the wound is his responsibility. The Prince generously allows Falstaff to take the credit for what he knows to be a false claim.

(d) 'I'll take it upon my death' is an oath, meaning 'May I die if I am not telling the truth'.

---

(2) Essay questions

The length required for an essay will vary, depending on the circumstances, but an indication of required length will usually be given. The specimen answers that follow assume an examination situation with limited time and no access to books. Essays written in the student's own time, with access to books, would generally be longer and include relevant quotations, with a clear indication of the source.

In all cases, whether under the pressure of limited time in an examination or not, you should plan an essay before writing it, to work out, in your head or in note form, the argument that is going to be put forward, the evidence to support it, and the order in which the various parts should be presented.

Examples are as follows:

(i) What significance does the episode of the robbery on Gad's Hill have in 1 Henry IV?

The story of the wild young Prince who robbed travellers on the highway was part of the legend that began to develop about Henry V in his own lifetime. *1 Henry IV*, though, makes significant changes to the traditional story. In Shakespeare's play the Prince refuses to take part in the robbery; he only consents to join Poins in the practical joke of robbing the robbers. We are also assured that the stolen money is repaid. Shakespeare makes the Prince a more responsible character than he was in the popular tradition. He also makes him a more complex character, to account for the conversion of the wild youth into the great king.

The scene also shows the breakdown of national morale. The system of authority in England has broken down. The King, Henry IV, is a usurper who has taken the crown by force from his cousin, the legitimate ruler, and bears responsibility for his death. If the highest office in the land can be taken by strong-arm methods then conventional values begin to be seen in a cynical way. Justice and honour and loyalty are shams; what is right is what strength or cunning can get away with. This is clearly stated in the conversation between Chamberlain and Gadshill at the inn before the robbery, with their talk of great men riding up and down on England, and making the commonwealth their 'boots'. The pun on 'boot' as both footwear and plunder is further extended in the suggestion that justice is corrupt, somebody's palm has been 'liquored', or as we would say, 'greased'. These robbers have little respect for the law when they see the King himself as a robber.

There is a parallel, too, between the robbers and the rebels. The Prince and Poins plot to take the proceeds of the robbery from Falstaff and the rest. Northumberland and Westmoreland (in the scene that follows the planning of the Gad's Hill robbery) involve Hotspur in their plot to take the kingdom of England from Henry IV; they had previously been Henry's supporters in taking it from Richard II. The tavern scene, in which the Prince and Falstaff and their companions celebrate their ill-gotten gains, is followed immediately by the scene in which the rebels propose the sharing of the booty—England—which they hope to win. There is yet another parallel worth mentioning too: Prince Henry carries off from the mock battle at Gad's Hill what Falstaff had taken from the travellers, and we may well believe that Falstaff knew whom he was fighting, as he later claimed. At the battle of Shrewsbury Falstaff takes away what the Prince has won, the honour due for killing Hotspur, and the Prince knows he is lying.

The robbery on Gad's Hill is Shakespeare's treatment of one of the stories of the wild youth of King Henry V. The episode has no part in the main action, the rebellion led by Hotspur. However, its relationship, in terms of parallels of action, with major events of the play, gives it thematic importance. It increases the play's social comment, and shows that all levels of society are involved in the breakdown of values that follows the murder of Richard II. It shows that rebels are robbers, whose real aim is to plunder the commonwealth. It does this by comic means that spread the range of the play's characters from ordinary working people, sympathetically presented, like the two Carriers, up to the King himself.

(ii) Discuss the relative importance, in 1 Henry IV, *of the characters of Prince Henry and Falstaff*

1 Henry IV was in Shakespeare's own day, and continues to be in ours, one of his most popular plays, and this popularity is a tribute to Falstaff, who is one of Shakespeare's greatest comic creations. Falstaff (as he says himself in *2 Henry IV*) is 'not only witty in himself, but the cause of wit that is in other men'. He is the butt of many jokes, but always his own wit turns the joke back on its maker, or his ingenuity finds a way out, or escape from the most difficult situations. 'By the Lord,' he answers Poins and the Prince, when challenged to explain why he ran away at Gad's Hill, 'I knew ye as well as he that made ye.' As a good subject he could not fight the Prince of Wales. This comic vigour makes us condone Falstaff's gross faults and he gives great pleasure to audiences.

In the wit-combats with Falstaff Prince Henry usually comes off second best, and there is often a harsh or condescending aspect to his humour, as in the exchange with the Drawer Francis. He has a serious part to play but it is not a popular part. The Prince is a reserved, cold and calculating character. Hotspur's passionate rhetoric, even though he is in the wrong in his commitment to rebellion, makes him a more sympathetic figure than the Prince, whose first significant speech (the soliloquy which closes I.2) announces his intention of playing a double part for political advantage.

But we are not merely concerned with popularity with an audience; at a more serious level of understanding, Prince Henry is central to the play, and of the utmost importance. The two parts of *Henry IV* are about the development of a successful ruler, and *Henry V* shows his achievement. The king who gives his name to *1 Henry IV* does not have a very large part. He is old, ill and remorseful, though still a strong and able ruler. He is one of the models for the Prince to follow; a man who is wily and unscrupulous and who, as the usurper of the throne and the man responsible for the death of his cousin, Richard II, the previous king, has a terrible crime on his conscience. On the other hand he is devoted to the welfare of England. King Henry holds Hotspur up as a model to the Prince. Hotspur is the soldier-hero, passionate in the pursuit of glory in arms. He is direct in speech, open and affectionate with friends and his wife, but he does not understand or care about the general good of the country. A third model for Prince Henry is Falstaff. He is clever, funny, and in his own way generous and humane. He is directed to the immediate and simple earthly pleasures, and lives in the present. But no community could survive on his principles; he can only be a parasite on the state.

Prince Henry follows none of these models but he takes something from each. He finds a way of giving order to the unruly impulses of Falstaff; he combines Hotspur's skill in arms with the King's sense of the deep obligations of a ruler to his people, and he does not inherit the King's guilt for the crime of Richard's death. Prince Henry is unquestionably the most important character in *1 Henry IV*.

Part 5

Suggestions for further reading

The text

HUMPHREYS, A. R. (ED.): *The First Part of King Henry IV* (The New Arden Shakespeare) Methuen, London, 1960, 1961, 1965. All line references in these notes are to this edition, the best available.

Other good editions are:

WILSON, J. D. (ED.): (The New Cambridge) Cambridge University Press, Cambridge, 1946.

FERGUSSON, F. AND SISSON, C. J. (ED.): (The Laurel Edition) Dell, New York, 1959.

MACK, MAYNARD (ED.): (The Signet Edition) New American Library, New York, 1965.

DAVISON, P. H. (ED.): (The New Penguin Edition) Penguin Books, Harmondsworth, 1968.

COLMER, J. A. AND COLMER, D.: (The New Swan Edition) Longman, London, 1965.

Related plays

The First Part of King Henry IV is the second in a series of four closely related plays which were planned as a sequence. It will certainly be more fully appreciated if it is read in conjunction with the other three plays. It is preceded by *Richard II* and followed by *The Second Part of King Henry IV* and *King Henry V*. Editions in the series listed above are available for these plays.

The anonymous play *Woodstock*, ed. A. P. Rossiter, Chatto and Windus, London, 1946, deals with the events immediately preceding Shakespeare's *Richard II*, and Rossiter's introduction is of interest.

General Reading

(a) Shakespeare's life:

SCHOENBAUM, S.: *Shakespeare's Lives*, Clarendon Press, Oxford, 1970. This examines all the documents and legends, and provides a useful guide to biographies.

(b) The theatre and players:

BALDWIN, T. W.: *Organization and Personnel of the Shakespearean Company*, Princeton University Press, Princeton, 1927: Russell, New York, 1961.

GURR, A.: *The Shakespearean Stage 1574–1642*, Cambridge University Press, Cambridge, 1970.

HODGES, C. W.: *The Globe Restored*, Ernest Benn, London, 1953; Oxford University Press, Oxford, 1968.

HOSLEY, R.: 'The Playhouses' in J. L. Barroll, A. Leggatt, R. Hosley and A. Kernan, *The Revels History of Drama in English, Vol. III 1576–1613*, Methuen, London, 1975.

(c) The history plays:

DORIUS, R. J.: *Discussions of Shakespeare's Histories*, Heath, Boston, 1964.

PRIOR, M. E.: *The Drama of Power: Studies in Shakespeare's History Plays*, North Western University Press, Evanston, Illinois, 1973.

RICHMOND, H. M.: *Shakespeare's Political Plays*, Random House, New York, 1967.

TILLYARD, E. M. W.: *The Elizabethan World Picture*, Chatto and Windus, London, 1943; 1958.

TILLYARD, E. M. W.: *Shakespeare's History Plays*, Chatto and Windus, London, 1944, 1956, 1961, 1964.

WAITH, E. M.: *Shakespeare: The Histories* (Twentieth Century Views), Prentice-Hall, Englewood Cliffs, New Jersey, 1965.

WILSON, J. D.: *The Fortunes of Falstaff*, Cambridge University Press, Cambridge, 1943, 1961.

The author of these notes

F. H. MARES was educated at the Universities of Durham and Oxford. On the completion of his BLITT in Oxford he was appointed Lecturer in English in the University of Western Australia in 1954; he moved to the University of Adelaide a few years later, where he worked until he retired (as Reader in English) at the end of 1985. He has been a Visiting Professor at the University of Michigan, the University of Virginia and at the University of Trondheim in Norway. He was elected a Fellow of the Australian Academy of the Humanities in 1974. His publications include the 'Revels' edition of *The Alchemist* by Ben Jonson (1967), *The Memoirs of Robert Carey* (Clarendon Press, 1972) and *Much Ado About Nothing* (Cambridge University Press, 1988).

York Notes: list of titles

CHINUA ACHEBE
A Man of the People
Arrow of God
Things Fall Apart
EDWARD ALBEE
Who's Afraid of Virginia Woolf?
ELECHI AMADI
The Concubine
ANONYMOUS
Beowulf
Everyman
AYI KWEI ARMAH
The Beautyful Ones Are Not Yet Born
W. H. AUDEN
Selected Poems
JANE AUSTEN
Emma
Mansfield Park
Northanger Abbey
Persuasion
Pride and Prejudice
Sense and Sensibility
HONORÉ DE BALZAC
Le Père Goriot
SAMUEL BECKETT
Waiting for Godot
SAUL BELLOW
Henderson, The Rain King
ARNOLD BENNETT
Anna of the Five Towns
The Card
WILLIAM BLAKE
Songs of Innocence, Songs of Experience
ROBERT BOLT
A Man For All Seasons
HAROLD BRIGHOUSE
Hobson's Choice
ANNE BRONTË
The Tenant of Wildfell Hall
CHARLOTTE BRONTË
Jane Eyre
EMILY BRONTË
Wuthering Heights
ROBERT BROWNING
Men and Women
JOHN BUCHAN
The Thirty-Nine Steps
JOHN BUNYAN
The Pilgrim's Progress
BYRON
Selected Poems
GEOFFREY CHAUCER
Prologue to the Canterbury Tales
The Clerk's Tale
The Franklin's Tale
The Knight's Tale
The Merchant's Tale
The Miller's Tale
The Nun's Priest's Tale
The Pardoner's Tale
The Wife of Bath's Tale
Troilus and Criseyde
SAMUEL TAYLOR COLERIDGE
Selected Poems
SIR ARTHUR CONAN DOYLE
The Hound of the Baskervilles

WILLIAM CONGREVE
The Way of the World
JOSEPH CONRAD
Heart of Darkness
Nostromo
Victory
STEPHEN CRANE
The Red Badge of Courage
BRUCE DAWE
Selected Poems
WALTER DE LA MARE
Selected Poems
DANIEL DEFOE
A Journal of the Plague Year
Moll Flanders
Robinson Crusoe
CHARLES DICKENS
A Tale of Two Cities
Bleak House
David Copperfield
Dombey and Son
Great Expectations
Hard Times
Little Dorrit
Oliver Twist
The Pickwick Papers
EMILY DICKINSON
Selected Poems
JOHN DONNE
Selected Poems
JOHN DRYDEN
Selected Poems
GERALD DURRELL
My Family and Other Animals
GEORGE ELIOT
Middlemarch
Silas Marner
The Mill on the Floss
T. S. ELIOT
Four Quartets
Murder in the Cathedral
Selected Poems
The Cocktail Party
The Waste Land
J. G. FARRELL
The Siege of Krishnapur
WILLIAM FAULKNER
Absalom, Absalom!
The Sound and the Fury
HENRY FIELDING
Joseph Andrews
Tom Jones
F. SCOTT FITZGERALD
Tender is the Night
The Great Gatsby
GUSTAVE FLAUBERT
Madame Bovary
E. M. FORSTER
A Passage to India
Howards End
JOHN FOWLES
The French Lieutenant's Woman
ATHOL FUGARD
Selected Plays
JOHN GALSWORTHY
Strife

MRS GASKELL
North and South
WILLIAM GOLDING
Lord of the Flies
The Spire
OLIVER GOLDSMITH
She Stoops to Conquer
The Vicar of Wakefield
ROBERT GRAVES
Goodbye to All That
GRAHAM GREENE
Brighton Rock
The Heart of the Matter
The Power and the Glory
WILLIS HALL
The Long and the Short and the Tall
THOMAS HARDY
Far from the Madding Crowd
Jude the Obscure
Selected Poems
Tess of the D'Urbervilles
The Mayor of Casterbridge
The Return of the Native
The Trumpet Major
The Woodlanders
Under the Greenwood Tree
L. P. HARTLEY
The Go-Between
The Shrimp and the Anemone
NATHANIEL HAWTHORNE
The Scarlet Letter
SEAMUS HEANEY
Selected Poems
JOSEPH HELLER
Catch-22
ERNEST HEMINGWAY
A Farewell to Arms
For Whom the Bell Tolls
The Old Man and the Sea
HERMANN HESSE
Steppenwolf
BARRY HINES
Kes
HOMER
The Iliad
The Odyssey
ANTHONY HOPE
The Prisoner of Zenda
GERARD MANLEY HOPKINS
Selected Poems
RICHARD HUGHES
A High Wind in Jamaica
TED HUGHES
Selected Poems
THOMAS HUGHES
Tom Brown's Schooldays
ALDOUS HUXLEY
Brave New World
HENRIK IBSEN
A Doll's House
Ghosts
HENRY JAMES
The Ambassadors
The Portrait of a Lady
Washington Square
SAMUEL JOHNSON
Rasselas
BEN JONSON
The Alchemist
Volpone
JAMES JOYCE
A Portrait of the Artist as a Young Man
Dubliners

JOHN KEATS
Selected Poems
PHILIP LARKIN
Selected Poems
D. H. LAWRENCE
Selected Short Stories
Sons and Lovers
The Rainbow
Women in Love
CAMARA LAYE
L'Enfant Noir
HARPER LEE
To Kill a Mocking-Bird
LAURIE LEE
Cider with Rosie
THOMAS MANN
Tonio Kröger
CHRISTOPHER MARLOWE
Doctor Faustus
ANDREW MARVELL
Selected Poems
W. SOMERSET MAUGHAM
Selected Short Stories
GAVIN MAXWELL
Ring of Bright Water
J. MEADE FALKNER
Moonfleet
HERMAN MELVILLE
Moby Dick
THOMAS MIDDLETON
Women Beware Women
THOMAS MIDDLETON and WILLIAM ROWLEY
The Changeling
ARTHUR MILLER
A View from the Bridge
Death of a Salesman
The Crucible
JOHN MILTON
Paradise Lost I & II
Paradise Lost IV & IX
Selected Poems
V. S. NAIPAUL
A House for Mr Biswas
ROBERT O'BRIEN
Z for Zachariah
SEAN O'CASEY
Juno and the Paycock
GABRIEL OKARA
The Voice
EUGENE O'NEILL
Mourning Becomes Electra
GEORGE ORWELL
Animal Farm
Nineteen Eighty-four
JOHN OSBORNE
Look Back in Anger
WILFRED OWEN
Selected Poems
ALAN PATON
Cry, The Beloved Country
THOMAS LOVE PEACOCK
Nightmare Abbey and Crotchet Castle
HAROLD PINTER
The Caretaker
SYLVIA PLATH
Selected Works
PLATO
The Republic
ALEXANDER POPE
Selected Poems

J. B. PRIESTLEY
  An Inspector Calls
THOMAS PYNCHON
  The Crying of Lot 49
SIR WALTER SCOTT
  Ivanhoe
  Quentin Durward
  The Heart of Midlothian
  Waverley
PETER SHAFFER
  The Royal Hunt of the Sun
WILLIAM SHAKESPEARE
  A Midsummer Night's Dream
  Antony and Cleopatra
  As You Like It
  Coriolanus
  Cymbeline
  Hamlet
  Henry IV Part I
  Henry IV Part II
  Henry V
  Julius Caesar
  King Lear
  Love's Labour's Lost
  Macbeth
  Measure for Measure
  Much Ado About Nothing
  Othello
  Richard II
  Richard III
  Romeo and Juliet
  Sonnets
  The Merchant of Venice
  The Taming of the Shrew
  The Tempest
  The Winter's Tale
  Troilus and Cressida
  Twelfth Night
GEORGE BERNARD SHAW
  Androcles and the Lion
  Arms and the Man
  Caesar and Cleopatra
  Candida
  Major Barbara
  Pygmalion
  Saint Joan
  The Devil's Disciple
MARY SHELLEY
  Frankenstein
PERCY BYSSHE SHELLEY
  Selected Poems
RICHARD BRINSLEY SHERIDAN
  The School for Scandal
  The Rivals
R. C. SHERRIFF
  Journey's End
WOLE SOYINKA
  The Road
EDMUND SPENSER
  The Faerie Queene (Book I)
JOHN STEINBECK
  Of Mice and Men
  The Grapes of Wrath
  The Pearl

LAURENCE STERNE
  A Sentimental Journey
  Tristram Shandy
ROBERT LOUIS STEVENSON
  Kidnapped
  Treasure Island
TOM STOPPARD
  Professional Foul
  Rosencrantz and Guildenstern are Dead
JONATHAN SWIFT
  Gulliver's Travels
JOHN MILLINGTON SYNGE
  The Playboy of the Western World
TENNYSON
  Selected Poems
W. M. THACKERAY
  Vanity Fair
DYLAN THOMAS
  Under Milk Wood
FLORA THOMPSON
  Lark Rise to Candleford
J. R. R. TOLKIEN
  The Hobbit
ANTHONY TROLLOPE
  Barchester Towers
MARK TWAIN
  Huckleberry Finn
  Tom Sawyer
JOHN VANBRUGH
  The Relapse
VIRGIL
  The Aeneid
VOLTAIRE
  Candide
KEITH WATERHOUSE
  Billy Liar
EVELYN WAUGH
  Decline and Fall
JOHN WEBSTER
  The Duchess of Malfi
H. G. WELLS
  The History of Mr Polly
  The Invisible Man
  The War of the Worlds
OSCAR WILDE
  The Importance of Being Earnest
THORNTON WILDER
  Our Town
TENNESSEE WILLIAMS
  The Glass Menagerie
VIRGINIA WOOLF
  Mrs Dalloway
  To the Lighthouse
WILLIAM WORDSWORTH
  Selected Poems
WILLIAM WYCHERLEY
  The Country Wife
W. B. YEATS
  Selected Poems

York Handbooks: list of titles

YORK HANDBOOKS form a companion series to York Notes and are designed to meet the wider needs of students of English and related fields. Each volume is a compact study of a given subject area, written by an authority with experience in communicating the essential ideas to students at all levels.